CCNP SWITCH
Portable Command Guide

Scott Empson
Hans Roth

Cisco Press

800 East 96th Street
Indianapolis, IN 46240 USA

CCNP SWITCH Portable Command Guide

Scott Empson

Hans Roth

Copyright© 2010 Cisco Systems, Inc.

Published by:
Cisco Press
800 East 96th Street
Indianapolis, IN 46240 USA

Printed in the United States of America

First Printing March 2010

Library of Congress Cataloging-in-Publication data is on file.

ISBN-13: 978-1-58720-248-3

ISBN-10: 1-58720-248-4

Warning and Disclaimer

This book is designed to provide information about the CCNP SWITCH exam (642-813). Every effort has been made to make this book as complete and as accurate as possible, but no warranty or fitness is implied.

The information is provided on an "as is" basis. The authors, Cisco Press, and Cisco Systems, Inc. shall have neither liability nor responsibility to any person or entity with respect to any loss or damages arising from the information contained in this book or from the use of the discs or programs that may accompany it.

The opinions expressed in this book belong to the author and are not necessarily those of Cisco Systems, Inc.

Trademark Acknowledgments

All terms mentioned in this book that are known to be trademarks or service marks have been appropriately capitalized. Cisco Press or Cisco Systems, Inc., cannot attest to the accuracy of this information. Use of a term in this book should not be regarded as affecting the validity of any trademark or service mark.

Corporate and Government Sales

The publisher offers excellent discounts on this book when ordered in quantity for bulk purchases or special sales, which may include electronic versions and/or custom covers and content particular to your business, training goals, marketing focus, and branding interests. For more information, please contact:

U.S. Corporate and Government Sales
1-800-382-3419 corpsales@pearsontechgroup.com

For sales outside the United States please contact:
International Sales international@pearsoned.com

Feedback Information

At Cisco Press, our goal is to create in-depth technical books of the highest quality and value. Each book is crafted with care and precision, undergoing rigorous development that involves the unique expertise of members from the professional technical community.

Readers' feedback is a natural continuation of this process. If you have any comments regarding how we could improve the quality of this book, or otherwise alter it to better suit your needs, you can contact us through e-mail at feedback@ciscopress.com. Please make sure to include the book title and ISBN in your message.

We greatly appreciate your assistance.

Publisher	Paul Boger
Associate Publisher	Dave Dusthimer
Cisco Representative	Erik Ullanderson
Cisco Press Program Manager	Anand Sundaram
Executive Editor	Mary Beth Ray
Managing Editor	Patrick Kanouse
Development Editor	Andrew Cupp
Senior Project Editor	Tonya Simpson
Copy Editor	Kelly Maish
Technical Editor	Sean Wilkins
Editorial Assistant	Vanessa Evans
Book Designer	Louisa Adair
Cover Designer	Sandra Schroeder
Composition	Mark Shirar
Proofreader	Sheri Cain

Americas Headquarters	Asia Pacific Headquarters	Europe Headquarters
Cisco Systems, Inc.	Cisco Systems (USA) Pte. Ltd.	Cisco Systems International BV
San Jose, CA	Singapore	Amsterdam, The Netherlands

Cisco has more than 200 offices worldwide. Addresses, phone numbers, and fax numbers are listed on the Cisco Website at www.cisco.com/go/offices.

CCDE, CCENT, Cisco Eos, Cisco HealthPresence, the Cisco logo, Cisco Lumin, Cisco Nexus, Cisco StadiumVision, Cisco TelePresence, Cisco WebEx, DCE, and Welcome to the Human Network are trademarks; Changing the Way We Work, Live, Play, and Learn and Cisco Store are service marks; and Access Registrar, Aironet, AsyncOS, Bringing the Meeting To You, Catalyst, CCDA, CCDP, CCIE, CCIP, CCNA, CCNP, CCSP, CCVP, Cisco, the Cisco Certified Internetwork Expert logo, Cisco IOS, Cisco Press, Cisco Systems, Cisco Systems Capital, the Cisco Systems logo, Cisco Unity, Collaboration Without Limitation, EtherFast, EtherSwitch, Event Center, Fast Step, Follow Me Browsing, FormShare, GigaDrive, HomeLink, Internet Quotient, IOS, iPhone, iQuick Study, IronPort, the IronPort logo, LightStream, Linksys, MediaTone, MeetingPlace, MeetingPlace Chime Sound, MGX, Networkers, Networking Academy, Network Registrar, PCNow, PIX, PowerPanels, ProConnect, ScriptShare, SenderBase, SMARTnet, Spectrum Expert, StackWise, The Fastest Way to Increase Your Internet Quotient, TransPath, WebEx, and the WebEx logo are registered trademarks of Cisco Systems, Inc. and/or its affiliates in the United States and certain other countries.

All other trademarks mentioned in this document or website are the property of their respective owners. The use of the word partner does not imply a partnership relationship between Cisco and any other company. (0812R)

About the Authors

Scott Empson is the associate chair of the Bachelor of Applied Information Systems Technology degree program at the Northern Alberta Institute of Technology in Edmonton, Alberta, Canada, where he teaches Cisco routing, switching, and network design courses in a variety of different programs—certificate, diploma, and applied degree—at the postsecondary level. Scott is also the program coordinator of the Cisco Networking Academy Program at NAIT, a Regional Academy covering central and northern Alberta. He has earned three undergraduate degrees: a Bachelor of Arts, with a major in English; a Bachelor of Education, again with a major in English/Language Arts; and a Bachelor of Applied Information Systems Technology, with a major in Network Management. Scott is currently completing his Master of Education from the University of Portland. He holds several industry certifications, including CCNP, CCAI, Network+, and CIEH. Prior to instructing at NAIT, he was a junior/senior high school English/Language Arts/Computer Science teacher at different schools throughout Northern Alberta. Scott lives in Edmonton, Alberta, with his wife, Trina, and two children, Zachariah and Shaelyn.

Hans Roth is an instructor in the electrical engineering technology department at Red River College in Winnipeg, Manitoba, Canada. Hans has been with the college for 13 years and teaches in both the engineering technology and IT areas. He has been with the Cisco Networking Academy since 2000, teaching CCNP curricula. Previous to teaching, Hans spent 15 years in R&D/product development designing microcontroller-based control systems for consumer products as well as for the automotive and agricultural industries.

About the Technical Reviewer

Sean Wilkins is an accomplished networking consultant and has been in the field of IT since the mid-1990s, working with companies such as Cisco, Lucent, Verizon, AT&T, and several other private companies. Sean currently holds certifications with Cisco (CCNP/ CCDP), Microsoft (MCSE), and CompTIA (A+ and Network+). He also has a Master of Science degree in information technology with a focus in network architecture and design, a Master's certificate in network security, a Bachelor of Science degree in computer networking, and an Associate of Applied Science degree in computer information systems. In addition to working as a consultant, Sean spends a lot of his time as a technical writer and editor for various companies.

Dedications

This book is again dedicated to my wonderful family—Trina, Zach, and Shae. Working on these books as well as my master's classes took me away from you all too often, and I thank you for all of your love and support.

—Scott

I'd like to again thank my wife, Carol, and daughter, Tess, for their constant support and understanding during those times I've spent cloistered in the basement writing.

—Hans

Acknowledgments

Anyone who has ever had anything to do with the publishing industry knows that it takes many, many people to create a book. Our names might be on the cover, but there is no way that we can take credit for all that occurred to get this book from idea to publication.

From Scott Empson: To the team at Cisco Press, once again you amaze me with your professionalism and the ability to make me look good. Paul, Dave, Mary Beth, Drew, Tonya, and Dayna—thank you for your continued support and belief in my little engineering journal.

Also with Cisco Press, a huge thank you to the marketing and publicity staff—Kourtnaye, Doug, and Jamie, as well as Kristin, Curt, and Emily. Without your hard work, no one would even know about these books, and for that I thank you (as does my wife and her credit card companies).

To my technical reviewer, Sean Wilkins—thanks for keeping me on track and making sure that what I wrote was correct and relevant.

A big thank you goes to my co-author, Hans Roth, for helping me through this with all of your technical expertise and willingness to assist in trying to make my ideas a reality.

From Hans Roth: The writing part of this process is only the tip of the iceberg. The overall effort is large and the involvement is wide to get any book completed. Working with you folks at Cisco Press has again been a wonderful partnership. Your ongoing professionalism, understanding, and patience have consistently helped me do a little better each time I sit down to write. Thank you, Mary Beth, Chris, Patrick, Drew, and Dayna.

To the technical reviewer, Sean Wilkins, thank you for your clarifications and questions.

Thank you, Scott, for your positive approach and energy, your attention to technical detail, your depth of expertise, as well as your "let's do it now!" method. It's always a great pleasure to try to keep up with you.

Contents at a Glance

Contents

Command Syntax Conventions

The conventions used to present command syntax in this book are the same conventions used in the IOS Command Reference. The Command Reference describes these conventions as follows:

- **Boldface** indicates commands and keywords that are entered literally as shown. In actual configuration examples and output (not general command syntax), boldface indicates commands that are manually input by the user (such as a **show** command).
- *Italic* indicates arguments for which you supply actual values.
- Vertical bars (|) separate alternative, mutually exclusive elements.
- Square brackets ([ ]) indicate an optional element.
- Braces ({ }) indicate a required choice.
- Braces within brackets ([{ }]) indicate a required choice within an optional element.

Introduction

Welcome to *CCNP SWITCH Portable Command Guide*. When Cisco Press approached me about updating the four-volume *CCNP Portable Command Guides*, two thoughts immediately jumped into my head: "Is it time for revisions already?" and "Yikes! I am in the middle of pursuing my master's degree. Where will I find the time?" Because of those thoughts, two more soon followed: "I wonder what Hans is up to?" and "I hope Carol is in a good mood, as I am about to ask to take Hans away again…." The result is what you now have before you: a new *Portable Command Guide* for the latest version of the CCNP exam that focuses on switching: CCNP SWITCH.

For those of you who have worked with my books before, thank you for looking at this one. I hope that it will help you as you prepare for the vendor exam, or assist you in your daily activities as a Cisco network administrator/manager.

For those of you who are new to my books, you are reading what is essentially a cleaned-up version of my own personal engineering journals—a small notebook that I carry around with me that contains little nuggets of information; commands that I use but then forget; IP address schemes for the parts of the network I work with only occasionally; and quick refreshers for those concepts that I work with only once or twice a year. Although I teach these topics to postsecondary students, the classes I teach sometimes occur only once a year; as you can attest to, it is extremely difficult to remember all those commands all the time. Having a journal of commands at your fingertips, without having to search the Cisco website, can be a real time-saver (or a job-saver if the network is down and you are responsible for getting it back online).

With the creation of the new CCNP exam objectives, there is always something new to read, or a new podcast to listen to, or another slideshow from CiscoLive that you missed or want to review. The engineering journal can be that central repository of information that won't weigh you down as you carry it from the office or cubicle to the server and infrastructure rooms in some remote part of the building or some branch office.

To make this guide a more realistic one for you to use, the folks at Cisco Press have decided to continue with an appendix of blank pages—pages on which you can write your own personal notes, such as your own configurations, commands that are not in this book but are needed in your world, and so on. That way, this book will look less like the authors' journals and more like your own.

Networking Devices Used in the Preparation of This Book

To verify the commands that are in this new series of *CCNP Portable Command Guides*, many different devices were used. The following is a list of the equipment used in the preparation of these books:

- C2620 router running Cisco IOS Release 12.3(7)T, with a fixed Fast Ethernet interface, a WIC 2A/S serial interface card, and an NM-1E Ethernet interface
- C2811 ISR bundle with PVDM2, CMME, a WIC-2T, FXS and FXO VICs, running Cisco IOS Release 12.4(3g)
- C2821 ISR bundle with HWICD 9ESW, a WIC 2A/S, running 12.4(16) Advanced Security IOS

- WS-C3560-24-EMI Catalyst Switch, running Cisco IOS Release 12.2(25)SE
- WS-C3550-24-EMI Catalyst Switch, running Cisco IOS Release 12.1(9)EA1c
- WS-2960-24TT-L Catalyst Switch, running Cisco IOS Release 12.2(25)SE
- WS-2950-12 Catalyst Switch, running version C2950-C3.0(5.3)WC(1) Enterprise Edition Software
- WS-C3750-24TS Catalyst Switches, running ipservicesk9 release 12.2(52)SE
- C1760-V Voice Router with PVDM-256K-20, WIC-4ESW, VIC-2FXO, VIC-2FXS running ENTSERVICESK9 release 12.4(11)T2

You might notice that some of the devices were not running the latest and greatest IOS. Some of them are running code that is quite old.

Those of you familiar with Cisco devices will recognize that a majority of these commands work across the entire range of the Cisco product line. These commands are not limited to the platforms and IOS versions listed. In fact, in most cases, these devices are adequate for someone to continue their studies beyond the CCNP level as well. We have endeavored to identify throughout the book commands that are specific to a platform and/or IOS version.

Who Should Read This Book?

This book is for those people preparing for the CCNP SWITCH exam, whether through self-study, on-the-job training and practice, study within the Cisco Academy Program, or study through the use of a Cisco Training Partner. This book includes some handy hints and tips along the way to make life a bit easier for you in this endeavor. It is small enough that you will find it easy to carry around with you. Big, heavy textbooks might look impressive on your bookshelf in your office, but can you really carry them all around with you when you are working in a server room or equipment closet somewhere?

Strategies for Exam Preparation

The strategy that you use for CCNP SWITCH might be slightly different from strategies that other readers use, mainly based on the skills, knowledge, and experience you already have obtained. For example, if you have attended the SWITCH course, you might take a different approach than someone who learned routing via on-the-job training.

Regardless of the strategy you use or the background you have, the book is designed to help you get to the point where you can pass the exam with the least amount of time required. For instance, there is no need for you to practice or read about VLANs or Spanning Tree if you fully understand it already. However, many people like to make sure they truly know a topic, and thus read over material they already know. Several book features help you gain the confidence you need to be convinced that you know some material already, and determine which topics you need to study more.

Organization of This Book

Although this book could be read cover to cover, we strongly advise against it. The book is designed to be a simple listing of those commands that you need to understand to pass the SWITCH exam. Very little theory is included in the Portable Command Guides; they are designed to list commands needed at this level of study.

This book roughly follows the list of objectives for the CCNP SWITCH exam:

- **Chapter 1: "Analyzing Campus Network Designs"**—This chapter shows the Cisco Hierarchical Model of Network Design; the Cisco Enterprise Composite Network Model, the Cisco Service-Oriented Network Architecture (SONA), and the PPDIOO network lifecycle.

- **Chapter 2: "Implementing VLANs in a Campus Network"**—This chapter provides information on creating, verifying, and troubleshooting Virtual LANs, along with private VLANs and EtherChannel.

- **Chapter 3: "Implementing Spanning Tree"**—This chapter provides information on the configuration of Spanning Tree, along with commands used to verify the protocol and to configure enhancements to Spanning Tree, such as Rapid Spanning Tree and Multiple Spanning Tree.

- **Chapter 4: "Implementing Inter-VLAN Routing"**—This chapter shows the different ways to enable inter-VLAN communication—using an external router or using SVIs on a multilayer switch. DHCP and CEF are also covered in this chapter.

- **Chapter 5: "Implementing a Highly Available Network"**—This chapter covers topics such as network logging and syslog, SNMP managed nodes, and Cisco IOS Service Level Agreements.

- **Chapter 6: "Implementing a First Hop Redundancy Protocols Solution"**—This chapter provides information needed to ensure you have first hop redundancy— HSRO, VRRP, and GLBP are covered here.

- **Chapter 7: "Minimizing Service Loss and Data Theft in a Campus Network"**— Security is the focus of this chapter. Topics covered include port security, 802.1x authentication, mitigating VLAN hopping, DHCP snooping, DAI, CDP security issues, LLDP configuration, SSH, restricting access to telnet as web interface sessions with ACLs, how to disable unneeded ports, and securing end-device access ports.

- **Chapter 8: "Accommodating Voice and Video in Campus Networks"**—This chapter covers topics such as configuring and verifying voice VLANs, Power over Ethernet (POE), High Availability for Voice and Video, and configuring and verifying AutoQoS.

- **Chapter 9: "Integrating Wireless LANs into a Campus Network"**—This chapter provides information on topics such as switch configuration for standalone APs and HREAPs as well as controller-based APs; configuration for a WLAN controller; configuration for WiSM controllers; and configuring a wireless client.

Did We Miss Anything?

As educators, we are always interested in hearing how our students, and now readers of our books, do on both vendor exams and future studies. If you would like to contact either of us and let us know how this book helped you in your certification goals, please do so. Did we miss anything? Let us know. Contact us at ccnpguide@empson.ca or through the Cisco Press website, www.ciscopress.com.

CHAPTER 1

Analyzing Campus Network Designs

This chapter provides information concerning the following network design requirement topics:

- Cisco Hierarchical Model of Network Design
- Cisco Enterprise Composite Network Model
- Cisco Service-Oriented Network Architecture
- PPDIOO Lifecycle Approach

No commands are associated with this module of the CCNP SWITCH Course Objectives.

Cisco Hierarchical Model of Network Design

Figure 1-1 shows the Cisco Hierarchical Network Model.

Figure 1-1   Cisco Hierarchical Network Model

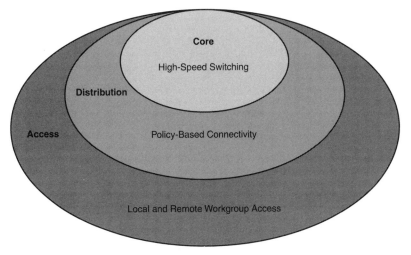

Layers in the Hierarchical Model

Core
High-Speed Switching

Distribution
Policy-Based Connectivity

Access

Local and Remote Workgroup Access

Cisco Enterprise Composite Network Model

Figure 1-2 shows the Cisco Enterprise Composite Network Model.

Figure 1-2   *Cisco Enterprise Composite Network Model*

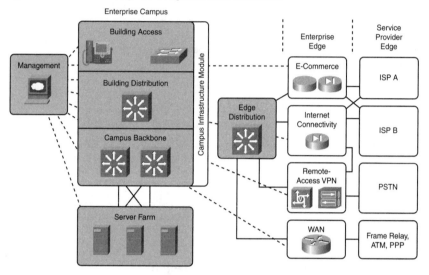

Cisco Service-Oriented Network Architecture

Figure 1-3 shows the Cisco Service-Oriented Network Architecture (SONA) framework.

Figure 1-3   Cisco Service-Oriented Network Architecture

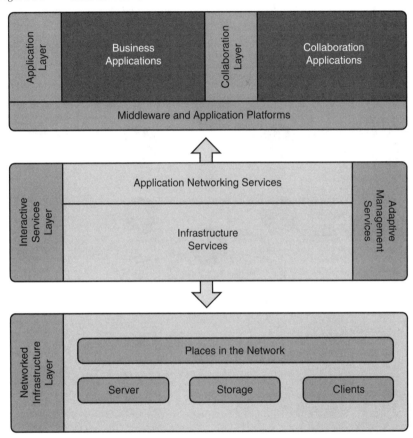

PPDIOO Lifecycle Approach

Figure 1-4 shows the Prepare, Plan, Design, Implement, Operate, and Optimize (PPDIOO) lifecycle.

Figure 1-4   Prepare, Plan, Design, Implement, Operate, and Optimize Lifecycle

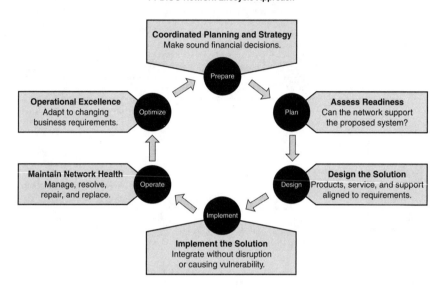

PPDIOO Network Lifecycle Approach

Implementing VLANs in a Campus Network

This chapter provides information and commands concerning the following topics:

Virtual LANs

- Creating static VLANs
    - Using VLAN-configuration mode
    - Using VLAN Database mode
- Assigning ports to VLANs
- Using the **range** command
- Dynamic Trunking Protocol (DTP)
- Setting the encapsulation type
- Verifying VLAN information
- Saving VLAN configurations
- Erasing VLAN configurations
- Verifying VLAN trunking
- VLAN Trunking Protocol (VTP)
    - Using VLAN Database mode
    - Using global configuration mode
- Verifying VTP

Private VLANs

- Configuring private VLANs (PVLAN)
- Configuring PVLAN trunks
- Verifying PVLANs
- Configuring protected ports

EtherChannel

- Configuring interface modes in EtherChannel
    - Without Port Aggregation Protocol (PAgP) or Link Aggregation Control Protocol (LACP)
    - With PAgP
    - With LACP
- Reviewing guidelines for configuring EtherChannel
- Configuring L2 EtherChannel
- Configuring L3 EtherChannel
- Verifying EtherChannel

- Configuring EtherChannel load balancing
- Determining the types of EtherChannel load balancing
- Verifying EtherChannel load balancing

Virtual Local Area Networks

This section covers creating static Virtual Local Area Networks (VLAN), assigning ports to VLANs, VLAN commands, DTP, setting the encapsulation type, verifying VLAN information, saving and erasing VLAN configurations, verifying VLAN trunking, and VLAN Trunking Protocol (VTP).

Creating Static VLANs

Static VLANs occur when the network administrator manually assigns a switch port to belong to a VLAN. Each port is associated with a specific VLAN. By default, all ports are originally assigned to VLAN 1. There are two different ways to create VLANs:

- Using the VLAN-configuration mode, which is the recommended method of creating VLANs
- Using the VLAN Database mode (which should not be used but is still available)

Using VLAN-Configuration Mode

`Switch(config)#`**`vlan 3`**	Creates VLAN 3 and enters VLAN-config mode for further definitions.
`Switch(config-vlan)#`**`name Engineering`**	Assigns a name to the VLAN. The length of the name can be from 1 to 32 characters.
`Switch(config-vlan)#`**`exit`**	Applies changes, increases the revision number by 1, and returns to global configuration mode.

NOTE: This method is the only way to configure extended-range VLANs (VLAN IDs from 1006–4094).

NOTE: Regardless of the method used to create VLANs, the VTP revision number is increased by one each time a VLAN is created or changed.

Using VLAN Database Mode

CAUTION: The VLAN Database mode has been deprecated and will be removed in some future Cisco IOS release. It is recommended to use only VLAN-configuration mode.

Switch#**vlan database**	Enters VLAN Database mode.
Switch(vlan)#**vlan 4 name Sales**	Creates VLAN 4 and names it Sales. The length of the name can be from 1 to 32 characters.
Switch(vlan)#**vlan 10**	Creates VLAN 10 and gives it a name of VLAN0010 as a default.
Switch(vlan)#**apply**	Applies changes to the VLAN database and increases the revision number by 1.
Switch(vlan)#**exit**	Applies changes to the VLAN database, increases the revision number by 1, and exits VLAN Database mode.

NOTE: You must apply the changes to the VLAN database for the changes to take effect. You must use either the **apply** command or the **exit** command to do so. Using the **exit** command applies the VLAN configurations and moves to the global configuration mode. Using the Ctrl-z command to exit out of the VLAN database does not work in this mode because it will abort all changes made to the VLAN database—you must either use **exit** or **apply** and then the **exit** command.

Assigning Ports to VLANs

Switch(config)#**interface fastethernet 0/1**	Moves to interface configuration mode
Switch(config-if)#**switchport mode access**	Sets the port to access mode
Switch(config-if)#**switchport access vlan 10**	Assigns this port to VLAN 10

NOTE: When the **switchport mode access** command is used, the port operates as a nontrunking, single VLAN interface that transmits and receives nonencapsulated frames.

An access port can belong to only one VLAN.

Using the **range** Command

`Switch(config)#interface range fastethernet 0/1 - 9`	Enables you to set the same configuration parameters on multiple ports at the same time.
	NOTE: There is a space before and after the hyphen in the **interface range** command.
`Switch(config-if-range)#switchport mode access`	Sets ports 1–9 as access ports.
`Switch(config-if-range)#switchport access vlan 10`	Assigns ports 1–9 to VLAN 10.

Dynamic Trunking Protocol

`Switch(config)#interface fastethernet 0/1`	Moves to interface configuration mode.
`Switch(config-if)#switchport mode dynamic desirable`	Makes the interface actively attempt to convert the link to a trunk link.
	NOTE: With the **switchport mode dynamic desirable** command set, the interface becomes a trunk link if the neighboring interface is set to **trunk**, **desirable**, or **auto**.
`Switch(config-if)#switchport mode dynamic auto`	Enables the interface to convert into a trunk link.
	NOTE: With the **switchport mode dynamic auto** command set, the interface becomes a trunk link if the neighboring interface is set to **trunk** or **desirable**.
`Switch(config-if)#switchport nonegotiate`	Prevents the interface from generating DTP frames.
	NOTE: Use the **switchport mode nonegotiate** command only when the interface switchport mode is **access** or **trunk**. You must manually configure the neighboring interface to establish a trunk link.

Switch(config-if)#**switchport mode trunk**	Puts the interface into permanent trunking mode and negotiates to convert the link into a trunk link.
	NOTE: With the **switchport mode trunk** command set, the interface becomes a trunk link even if the neighboring interface is not a trunk link.

NOTE: The default mode is dependent on the platform. For the 2960, 3560, and the 3760, the default mode is dynamic auto.

Setting the Encapsulation Type

3560Switch(config)#**interface fastethernet 0/1**	Moves to interface config mode.
3560Switch(config-if)#**switchport mode trunk**	Puts the interface into permanent trunking mode and negotiates to convert the link into a trunk link.
3560Switch(config-if)#**switchport trunk encapsulation isl**	Specifies Inter-Switch Link (ISL) encapsulation on the trunk link.
3560Switch(config-if)#**switchport trunk encapsulation dot1q**	Specifies 802.1Q encapsulation on the trunk link.
3560Switch(config-if)#**switchport trunk encapsulation negotiate**	Specifies that the interface negotiate with the neighboring interface to become either an ISL or Dot1Q trunk, depending on the capabilities or configuration of the neighboring interface.

TIP: With the **switchport trunk encapsulation negotiate** command set, the preferred trunking method is ISL.

CAUTION: The 2960 series switch supports only Dot1Q trunking.

Verifying VLAN Information

Switch#**show vlan**	Displays VLAN information
Switch#**show vlan brief**	Displays VLAN information in brief
Switch#**show vlan id 2**	Displays information of VLAN 2 only
Switch#**show vlan name marketing**	Displays information of VLAN named marketing only
Switch#**show interfaces vlan** *x*	Displays interface characteristics for the specified VLAN

Saving VLAN Configurations

The configurations of VLANs 1 through 1005 are always saved in the VLAN database. As long as the **apply** or **exit** command is executed in VLAN Database mode, changes are saved. If you are using VLAN-configuration mode, either the **exit** command or the Ctrl-z key sequence saves the changes to the VLAN database.

If you are using the VLAN database configuration at startup and the startup configuration file contains extended-range VLAN configuration, this information is lost when the system boots.

If you are using VTP transparent mode, the configurations are also saved in the running configuration and can be saved to the startup configuration using the **copy running-config startup-config** command.

If the VTP mode is transparent in the startup configuration, and the VLAN database and the VTP domain name from the VLAN database matches that in the startup configuration file, the VLAN database is ignored (cleared), and the VTP and VLAN configurations in the startup configuration file are used. The VLAN database revision number remains unchanged in the VLAN database.

Erasing VLAN Configurations

Switch#**delete flash:vlan.dat**	Removes the entire VLAN database from flash.
	CAUTION: Make sure there is *no* space between the colon (:) and the characters **vlan.dat**. You can potentially erase the entire contents of the flash with this command if the syntax is not correct. Make sure you read the output from the switch. If you need to cancel, press Ctrl-C to escape back to privileged mode: (Switch#) Switch#**delete flash:vlan.dat** Delete filename [vlan.dat]? Delete flash:vlan.dat? [confirm] Switch#
Switch(config)#**interface fastethernet 0/5**	Moves to interface config mode.
Switch(config-if)#**no switchport access vlan 5**	Removes port from VLAN 5 and reassigns it to VLAN 1—the default VLAN.
Switch(config-if)#**exit**	Moves to global config mode.
Switch(config)#**no vlan 5**	Removes VLAN 5 from the VLAN database.
or	
Switch#**vlan database**	Enters VLAN Database mode.
Switch(vlan)#**no vlan 5**	Removes VLAN 5 from the VLAN database.
Switch(vlan)#**exit**	Applies changes, increases the revision number by 1, and exits VLAN Database mode.

NOTE: When you delete a VLAN from a switch that is in VTP server mode, the VLAN is removed from the VLAN database for all switches in the VTP domain. When you delete a VLAN from a switch that is in VTP transparent mode, the VLAN is deleted only on that specific switch.

NOTE: You cannot delete the default VLANs for the different media types: Ethernet VLAN 1 and FDDI or Token Ring VLANs 1002 to 1005.

CAUTION: When you delete a VLAN, any ports assigned to that VLAN become inactive. They remain associated with the VLAN (and thus inactive) until you assign them to a new VLAN. Therefore, it is recommended that you reassign ports to a new VLAN or the default VLAN before you delete a VLAN from the VLAN database.

Verifying VLAN Trunking

`Switch#`**`show interface`** **`fastethernet 0/1 switchport`**	Displays the administrative and operational status of a trunking port

VLAN Trunking Protocol

VLAN Trunking Protocol (VTP) is a Cisco proprietary protocol that allows for VLAN configuration (addition, deletion, or renaming of VLANS) to be consistently maintained across a common administrative domain.

Using Global Configuration Mode

`Switch(config)#`**`vtp mode client`**	Changes the switch to VTP client mode.
`Switch(config)#`**`vtp mode server`**	Changes the switch to VTP server mode.
`Switch(config)#`**`vtp mode`** **`transparent`**	Changes the switch to VTP transparent mode.
	NOTE: By default, all Catalyst switches are in server mode.
`Switch(config)#`**`no vtp mode`**	Returns the switch to the default VTP server mode.
`Switch(config)#`**`vtp domain`** *`domain-`* *`name`*	Configures the VTP domain name. The name can be from 1 to 32 characters long.
	NOTE: All switches operating in VTP server or client mode must have the same domain name to ensure communication.
`Switch(config)#`**`vtp password`** *`password`*	Configures a VTP password. In Cisco IOS Software Release 12.3 and later, the password is an ASCII string from 1 to 32 characters long. If you are using a Cisco IOS release earlier than 12.3, the password length ranges from 8 to 64 characters long.
	NOTE: To communicate with each other, all switches must have the same VTP password set.

Switch(config)#**vtp v2-mode**	Sets the VTP domain to Version 2. This command is for Cisco IOS Software Release 12.3 and later. If you are using a Cisco IOS release earlier than 12.3, the command is **vtp version 2**.
	NOTE: VTP Versions 1 and 2 are not interoperable. All switches must use the same version. The biggest difference between Versions 1 and 2 is that Version 2 has support for Token Ring VLANs.
Switch(config)#**vtp pruning**	Enables VTP pruning.
	NOTE: By default, VTP pruning is disabled. You need to enable VTP pruning on only one switch in VTP server mode.

NOTE: Only VLANs included in the pruning-eligible list can be pruned. VLANs 2 through 1001 are pruning eligible by default on trunk ports. Reserved VLANs and extended-range VLANs cannot be pruned. To change which eligible VLANs can be pruned, use the interface-specific **switchport trunk pruning vlan** command:

```
Switch(config-if)#switchport trunk pruning vlan remove 4, 20-30
! Removes VLANs 4 and 20-30
Switch(config-if)#switchport trunk pruning vlan except 40-50
! All VLANs are added to the pruning list except for 40-50
```

Using VLAN Database Mode

CAUTION: The VLAN Database mode has been deprecated and will be removed in some future Cisco IOS release. Recommended practice dictates using only the VLAN-configuration mode.

Switch#**vlan database**	Enters VLAN Database mode.
Switch(vlan)#**vtp client**	Changes the switch to VTP client mode.
Switch(vlan)#**vtp server**	Changes the switch to VTP server mode.
Switch(vlan)#**vtp transparent**	Changes the switch to VTP transparent mode.
	NOTE: By default, all Catalyst switches are in server mode.

`Switch(vlan)#`**`vtp domain`** *`domain-name`*	Configures the VTP domain name. The name can be from 1 to 32 characters long.
	NOTE: All switches operating in VTP server or client mode must have the same domain name to ensure communication.
`Switch(vlan)#`**`vtp password`** *`password`*	Configures a VTP password. In Cisco IOS Release 12.3 and later, the password is an ASCII string from 1 to 32 characters long. If you are using a Cisco IOS release earlier than IOS 12.3, the password length ranges from 8 to 64 characters long.
	NOTE: All switches must have the same VTP password set to communicate with each other.
`Switch(vlan)#`**`vtp v2-mode`**	Sets the VTP domain to Version 2. This command is used in VLAN Database configuration mode. If you are configuring VTP version in global configuration mode, use the **vtp version 2** command.
	NOTE: VTP Versions 1 and 2 are not interoperable. All switches must use the same version. The biggest difference between Versions 1 and 2 is that Version 2 has support for Token Ring VLANs.
`Switch(vlan)#`**`vtp pruning`**	Enables VTP pruning.
	NOTE: By default, VTP pruning is disabled. You need to enable VTP pruning on only one switch in VTP server mode.

	NOTE: Only VLANs included in the pruning-eligible list can be pruned. VLANs 2 through 1001 are pruning eligible by default on trunk ports. Reserved VLANs and extended-range VLANs cannot be pruned. To change which eligible VLANs can be pruned, use the interface-specific **switchport trunk pruning vlan** command: `Switch(config-if)#`**`switchport trunk`** **`  pruning vlan remove 4, 20-30`** `! Removes VLANs 4 and 20-30` `Switch(config-if)#`**`switchport trunk`** **`  pruning vlan except 40-50`** All VLANs are added to the pruning list except for 40 through 50.
`Switch(vlan)#`**`exit`**	Applies changes to VLAN database, increases the revision number by 1, and exits back to privileged mode.

Verifying VTP

`Switch#`**`show vtp status`**	Displays general information about VTP configuration.
`Switch#`**`show vtp counters`**	Displays the VTP counters for the switch.

NOTE: If trunking has been established before VTP is set up, VTP information is propagated throughout the switch fabric almost immediately. However, because VTP information is advertised only every 300 seconds (5 minutes) unless a change has been made to force an update, it can take several minutes for VTP information to be propagated.

Configuration Example: VLANs

Figure 2-1 shows the network topology for the configuration that follows, which shows how to configure VLANs using the commands covered in this chapter.

Figure 2-1   Network Topology for VLAN Configuration Example

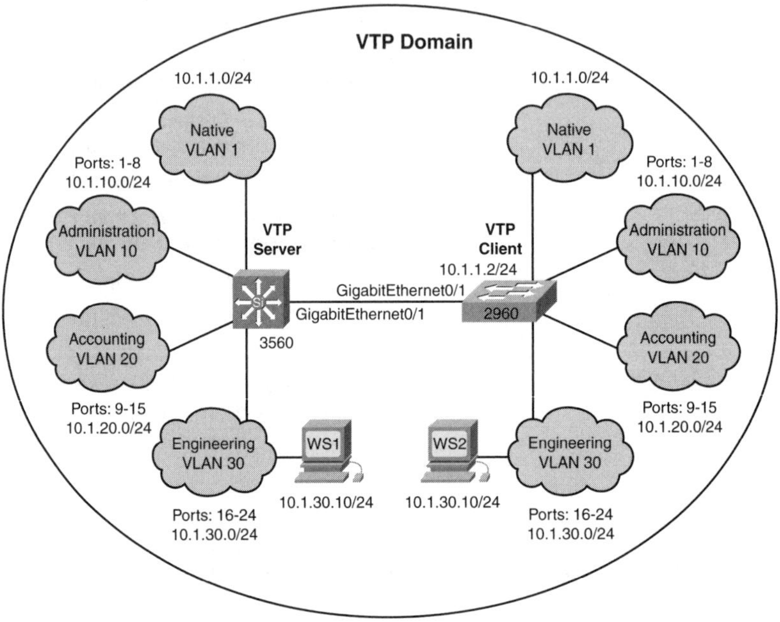

3560 Switch

Switch>**enable**	Moves to privileged mode.
Switch#**configure terminal**	Moves to global configuration mode.
Switch(config)#**hostname 3560**	Sets the host name.
3560(config)#**vtp mode server**	Changes the switch to VTP server mode. Note that **server** is the default setting for a 3560 switch.
3560(config)#**vtp domain southwest1**	Configures the VTP domain name to southwest1.
3560(config)#**vtp password tower**	Sets the VTP password to tower.
3560(config)#**vlan 10**	Creates VLAN 10 and enters VLAN-configuration mode.
3560(config-vlan)#**name Admin**	Assigns a name to the VLAN.

`3560(config-vlan)#exit`	Increases the revision number by 1 and returns to global configuration mode.
`3560(config)#vlan 20`	Creates VLAN 20 and enters VLAN-configuration mode.
`3560(config-vlan)#name Accounting`	Assigns a name to the VLAN.
`3560(config-vlan)#vlan 30`	Creates VLAN 30 and enters VLAN-configuration mode. Note that you do not have to exit back to global configuration mode to execute this command.
`3560(config-vlan)#name Engineering`	Assigns a name to the VLAN.
`3560(config-vlan)#exit`	Increases the revision number by 1 and returns to global configuration mode.
`3560(config)#interface range fasthethernet 0/1 - 8`	Enables you to set the same configuration parameters on multiple ports at the same time.
`3560(config-if-range)#switchport mode access`	Sets ports 1–8 as access ports.
`3560(config-if-range)#switchport access vlan 10`	Assigns ports 1–8 to VLAN 10.
`3560(config-if-range)#interface range fastethernet 0/9 - 15`	Enables you to set the same configuration parameters on multiple ports at the same time.
`3560(config-if-range)#switchport mode access`	Sets ports 9–15 as access ports.
`3560(config-if-range)#switchport access vlan 20`	Assigns ports 9–15 to VLAN 20.
`3560(config-if-range)#interface range fastethernet 0/16 - 24`	Enables you to set the same configuration parameters on multiple ports at the same time.
`3560(config-if-range)#switchport mode access`	Sets ports 16–24 as access ports.
`3560(config-if-range)#switchport access vlan 30`	Assigns ports 16–24 to VLAN 30.
`3560(config-if-range)#exit`	Returns to global configuration mode.

`3560(config)#interface gigabitethernet 0/1`	Moves to interface configuration mode.
`3560(config-if)#switchport trunk encapsulation dot1q`	Specifies 802.1Q encapsulation on the trunk link.
`3560(config-if)#switchport mode trunk`	Puts the interface into permanent trunking mode and negotiates to convert the link into a trunk link.
`3560(config-if)#exit`	Returns to global configuration mode.
`3560(config)#exit`	Returns to privileged mode.
`3560#copy running-config startup-config`	Saves the configuration in NVRAM.

2960 Switch

`Switch>enable`	Moves to privileged mode.
`Switch#configure terminal`	Moves to global configuration mode.
`Switch(config)#hostname 2960`	Sets the host name.
`2960(config)#vtp mode client`	Changes the switch to VTP client mode.
`2960(config)#vtp domain southwest1`	Configures the VTP domain name to southwest1.
`2960(config)#interface range fastethernet 0/1 - 8`	Enables you to set the same configuration parameters on multiple ports at the same time.
`2960(config-if-range)#switchport mode access`	Sets ports 1–8 as access ports.
`2960(config-if-range)#switchport access vlan 10`	Assigns ports 1–8 to VLAN 10.
`2960(config-if-range)#interface range fastethernet 0/9 - 15`	Enables you to set the same configuration parameters on multiple ports at the same time.
`2960(config-if-range)#switchport mode access`	Sets ports 9–15 as access ports.
`2960(config-if-range)#switchport access vlan 20`	Assigns ports 9–15 to VLAN 20.

`2960(config-if-range)#interface range fastethernet 0/16 - 24`	Enables you to set the same configuration parameters on multiple ports at the same time.
`2960(config-if-range)#switchport mode access`	Sets ports 16–24 as access ports.
`2960(config-if-range)#switchport access vlan 30`	Assigns ports 16–24 to VLAN 30.
`2960(config-if-range)#exit`	Returns to global configuration mode.
`2960(config)#interface gigabitethernet 0/1`	Moves to interface configuration mode.
`2960(config-if)#switchport mode trunk`	Puts the interface into permanent trunking mode and negotiates to convert the link into a trunk link.
`2960(config-if)#exit`	Returns to global configuration mode.
`2960(config)#exit`	Returns to privileged mode.
`2960#copy running-config startup-config`	Saves the configuration in NVRAM.

Private Virtual Local Area Networks

This section covers configuring private VLANs (PVLAN), configuring PVLAN trunks, verifying PVLANs, and configuring protected ports.

Configuring Private VLANs

A problem can potentially exist when an Internet service provider (ISP) has many devices from different customers on a single demilitarized zone (DMZ) segment or VLAN—these devices are not isolated from each other. Some switches can implement PVLANs, which keep some switch ports shared and some isolated, even though all ports are in the same VLAN. This isolation eliminates the need for a separate VLAN and IP subnet per customer.

NOTE: Private VLANs are implemented to varying degrees on Catalyst 6500/4500/3750/3560 as well as the Metro Ethernet line of switches. All PVLAN configuration commands are not supported on all switch platforms. For more information, see Appendix A, "Private VLAN Catalyst Switch Support Matrix."

`Switch(config)#`**`vtp mode`** **`transparent`**	Sets VTP mode to transparent.
`Switch(config)#`**`vlan 20`**	Creates VLAN 20 and moves to VLAN-configuration mode.
`Switch(config-vlan)#`**`private-vlan`** **`primary`**	Creates a private, primary VLAN.
`Switch(config-vlan)#`**`vlan 101`**	Creates VLAN 101 and moves to VLAN-config mode.
`Switch(config-vlan)#`**`private-vlan`** **`isolated`**	Creates a private, isolated VLAN for VLAN 101.
	NOTE: An isolated VLAN can communicate only with promiscuous ports.
`Switch(config-vlan)#`**`exit`**	Returns to global configuration mode.
`Switch(config)#`**`vlan 102`**	Creates VLAN 102 and moves to VLAN-config mode.
`Switch(config-vlan)#`**`private-vlan`** **`community`**	Creates a private, community VLAN for VLAN 102.
	NOTE: A community VLAN can communicate with all promiscuous ports and with other ports in the same community.
`Switch(config-vlan)#`**`exit`**	Returns to global config mode.
`Switch(config)#`**`vlan 103`**	Creates VLAN 103 and moves to VLAN-config mode.
`Switch(config-vlan)#`**`private-vlan`** **`community`**	Creates a private, community VLAN for VLAN 103.
`Switch(config-vlan)#`**`vlan 20`**	Returns to VLAN-config mode for VLAN 20.
`Switch(config-vlan)#`**`private-vlan`** **`association 101-103`**	Associates secondary VLANs 101–103 with primary VLAN 20.

	NOTE: Only one isolated VLAN can be mapped to a primary VLAN, but more than one community VLAN can be mapped to a primary VLAN.
`Switch(config)#interface fastethernet 0/20`	Moves to interface config mode
`Switch(config-if)#switchport mode private-vlan host`	Configures the port as a private VLAN host port.
`Switch(config-if)#switchport private-vlan host-association 20 101`	Associates the port with primary private VLAN 20 and secondary private VLAN 101.
`Switch(config-if)#exit`	Moves to global configuration mode.
`Switch(config)#interface fastethernet 0/21`	Moves to interface config mode.
`Switch(config-if)#switchport mode private-vlan promiscuous`	Configures the port as a private VLAN promiscuous port.
`Switch(config-if)#switchport private-vlan mapping 20 101 102 103`	Maps VLAN 20, 101, 102, and 103 to promiscuous port.

PVLAN Trunk on the Catalyst 3560/3750

`Switch(config)# interface fastethernet 0/23`	Moves to interface configuration mode.
`Switch(config-if)# switchport trunk encapsulation dot1q`	Specifies 802.1Q encapsulation on the trunk link.
`Switch(config-if)# switchport trunk native vlan 99`	Specifies the native VLAN as 99.
`Switch(config-if)# switchport mode trunk`	Puts the interface into permanent trunking mode and negotiates to convert the link into a trunk link.
	NOTE: Do not prohibit primary or secondary private VLANs on the trunk through policy or pruning.

PVLAN Trunk on the Catalyst 4500

This configuration shows how to configure interface FastEthernet 5/2 as a secondary trunk port.

Switch(config)# **interface fastethernet 5/2**	Moves to interface configuration mode.
Switch(config-if)# **switchport mode private-vlan trunk secondary**	Specifies that the ports with a valid PVLAN trunk association become active host private VLAN trunk ports.
Switch(config-if)# **switchport private-vlan trunk native vlan 10**	Specifies the native VLAN as 10.
Switch(config-if)# **switchport private-vlan trunk allowed vlan 10 3-4**	Enables the native VLAN 10 and VLANs 3–4 on the trunk.
Switch(config-if)# **switchport private-vlan association trunk 3 301**	Associates the secondary private VLAN 301 to the primary private VLAN 3.

PVLAN on a 3750 Layer 3 Switch

The Catalyst 3750 can provide private VLANs when operating as a Layer 3 switch. The Switch Virtual Interface (SVI) is the primary VLAN. The secondary VLANs are mapped at the SVI instead of at the promiscuous port. All other configuration, including creating and configuring primary and secondary VLANs and applying those VLANs to switch ports, remains the same.

Switch(config)# **interface Vlan100**	Moves to interface configuration mode.
Switch(config-if)# **ip address 172.20.100.1 255.255.255.0**	Specifies an IP address for SVI interface VLAN 1.
Switch(config-if)# **private-vlan mapping 101-102**	Maps the secondary VLANs 101 and 102 to the Layer 3 interface VLAN 1.
	NOTE: Dynamic or static routing must be configured.

Verifying PVLANs

Switch#**show vlan private-vlan type**	Verifies private VLAN configuration.
Switch#**show interface fastethernet 0/20 switchport**	Verifies all configuration on fastethernet 0/20, including private VLAN associations.

Configuration Example: PVLAN

Figure 2-2 shows the network topology for the configuration that follows, which shows how to configure PVLANs using the commands covered in this chapter. The following network functionality is required:

- DNS, WWW, and SMTP are in server farm, same subnet.
- WWW and SMTP servers can communicate only with router.
- DNS servers can communicate with each other and with router.
- The servers are attached to two switches.
- One switch is required to route traffic (L3) from the servers.

Figure 2-2   Network Topology for PVLAN Configuration Example

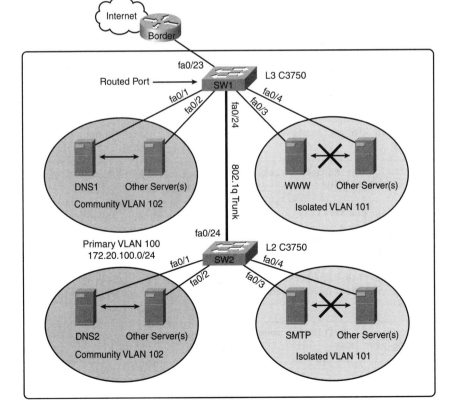

Switch SW1

Switch(config)#**hostname SW1**	Names the switch SW1.
SW1(config)#**vtp mode transparent**	Specifies the VTP device mode as transparent.
SW1(config)#**ip dhcp pool 172_20_100**	Creates a DHCP pool named 172_20_100.
SW1(dhcp-config)#**network 172.20.100.0 255.255.255.0**	Provides IP addresses for DHCP clients in the 172.20.100.0/24 network.
SW1(dhcp-config)#**default-router 172.20.100.1**	Defines the default gateway for the DHCP clients.
SW1(dhcp-config)#**exit**	Exits DHCP configuration mode.
SW1(config)#**ip dhcp excluded-address 172.20.100.1 172.20.100.63**	Excludes the first 64 IP addresses from the DHCP scope.
SW1(config-vlan)#**vlan 101**	Creates VLAN 101.
SW1(config-vlan)#**private-vlan isolated**	Defines the VLAN 101 as private and having isolated ports.
SW1(config-vlan)#**vlan 102**	Creates VLAN 102.
SW1(config-vlan)#**private-vlan community**	Defines VLAN 102 as private and having community ports.
SW1(config)#**vlan 100**	Creates VLAN 100.
SW1(config-vlan)#**private-vlan primary**	Defines VLAN 100 as the primary VLAN for the private VLANs.
SW1(config-vlan)#**private-vlan association 101-102**	Associates the secondary VLANs to the primary VLAN 100.
SW1(config-vlan)#**exit**	Exits VLAN configuration mode.
SW1(config)#**interface FastEthernet0/1 - 2**	Moves to interface range configuration mode.
SW1(config-if)#**switchport private-vlan host-association 100 101**	Defines the switch ports as private and associated with primary VLAN 100 and secondary (isolated) VLAN 101.
SW1(config-if)#**switchport mode private-vlan host**	Configures the interfaces as private-VLAN host ports.

SW1(config)#**interface FastEthernet0/3 - 4**	Moves to interface range configuration mode.
SW1(config-if)#**switchport private-vlan host-association 100 102**	Defines the switch ports as private and associated with primary VLAN 100 and secondary (community) VLAN 102.
SW1(config-if)#**switchport mode private-vlan host**	Configures the interfaces as private-VLAN host ports.
SW1(config)#**interface FastEthernet0/23**	Moves to interface configuration mode.
SW1(config-if)#**no switchport**	Sets the interface to the routed-interface status.
SW1(config-if)#**ip address 172.19.100.10 255.255.255.0**	Applies an IP address to the routed interface.
SW1(config)#**interface FastEthernet0/24**	Moves to interface configuration mode.
SW1(config-if)#**switchport trunk encapsulation dot1q**	Sets the interface to an 802.1q trunk.
	NOTE: This trunk connects the primary and secondary PVLANs between SW1 and SW2. Only IEEE 802.1q encapsulation is supported.
SW1(config-if)#**switchport mode trunk**	Sets the port to trunk unconditionally.
	NOTE: Do not prohibit primary or secondary private VLANs on the trunk through policy or pruning.
SW1(config)#**interface Vlan100**	Creates an SVI for the primary private VLAN.
SW1(config-if)#**ip address 172.20.100.1 255.255.255.0**	Applies an IP address to the SVI.
SW1(config-if)#**private-vlan mapping 101-102**	Maps both secondary PVLANs to the SVI VLAN 100.
SW1(config)#**ip route 0.0.0.0 0.0.0.0 172.19.100.1**	Creates a candidate default route to the corporate BORDER router.

Switch SW2

`Switch(config)#`**`hostname SW2`**	Names the switch SW2.
`SW2(config)#`**`vtp mode transparent`**	Specifies the VTP device mode as transparent.
`SW2(config)#`**`vlan 101`**	Creates VLAN 101.
`SW2(config-vlan)#`**`private-vlan isolated`**	Defines the VLAN 101 as private with isolated ports.
`SW2(config-vlan)#`**`vlan 102`**	Creates VLAN 102.
`SW2(config-vlan)#`**`private-vlan community`**	Defines VLAN 102 as private with community ports.
`SW2(config)#`**`vlan 100`**	Creates VLAN 100.
`SW2(config-vlan)#`**`private-vlan primary`**	Defines VLAN 100 as the primary VLAN for the private VLANs.
`SW2(config-vlan)#`**`private-vlan association 101-102`**	Associates the secondary VLANs to the primary VLAN.
`SW2(config)#`**`interface FastEthernet0/1 - 2`**	Moves to interface range configuration mode.
`SW2(config-if)#`**`switchport private-vlan host-association 100 101`**	Defines the switch ports as private and associated with primary VLAN 100 and secondary VLAN 101.
`SW2(config-if)#`**`switchport mode private-vlan host`**	Configures the interfaces as private-VLAN host ports.
`SW2(config)#`**`interface FastEthernet0/3 - 4`**	Moves to interface range configuration mode.
`SW2(config-if)#`**`switchport private-vlan host-association 100 102`**	Defines the switch ports as private and associated with primary VLAN 100 and secondary VLAN 102.
`SW2(config-if)#`**`switchport mode private-vlan host`**	Configures the interfaces as private-VLAN host ports.
`SW2(config)#`**`interface FastEthernet0/24`**	Moves to interface configuration mode.
`SW2(config-if)#`**`switchport trunk encapsulation dot1q`**	Sets the interface to an 802.1q trunk.

	NOTE: This trunk connects the primary and secondary PVLANs between SW1 and SW2. Only IEEE 802.1q encapsulation is supported.
SW2(config-if)#**switchport mode trunk**	Sets the port to trunk unconditionally.
SW2(config-if)#**switchport mode private-vlan promiscuous**	Sets the trunk port to promiscuous mode.
SW2(config-if)#**switchport private-vlan mapping 100 101-102**	Maps VLANs 100, 101, and 102 to the promiscuous port.

EtherChannel

EtherChannel provides fault-tolerant high-speed links among switches, routers, and servers. An EtherChannel consists of individual Fast Ethernet or Gigabit Ethernet links bundled into a single logical link. If a link within an EtherChannel fails, traffic previously carried over that failed link changes to the remaining links within the EtherChannel.

Interface Modes in EtherChannel

Mode	Protocol	Description
On	None	Forces the interface into an EtherChannel without PAgP or LACP. Channel exists only if connected to another interface group also in On mode.
Auto	PAgP	Places the interface into a passive negotiating state—will respond to PAgP packets but will not initiate PAgP negotiation.
Desirable	PAgP	Places the interface into an active negotiating state—will send PAgP packets to start negotiations.
Passive	LACP	Places the interface into a passive negotiating state—will respond to LACP packets but will not initiate LACP negotiation.
Active	LACP	Places the interface into an active negotiating state—will send LACP packets to start negotiations.

Guidelines for Configuring EtherChannel
- PAgP is Cisco proprietary.
- LACP is defined in 802.3ad.

- Can combine from two to eight parallel links.
- All ports must be identical:
  — Same speed and duplex
  — Cannot mix Fast Ethernet and Gigabit Ethernet
  — Cannot mix PAgP and LACP
  — Must all be VLAN trunk or nontrunk operational status
- All links must be either L2 or L3 in a single channel group.
- To create a channel in PAgP, sides must be set to
  — Auto-Desirable
  — Desirable-Desirable
- To create a channel in LACP, sides must be set to
  — Active-Active
  — Active-Passive
- To create a channel without using PAgP or LACP, sides must be set to On-On.
- Do not configure a GigaStack Gigabit Interface Converter (GBIC) as part of an EtherChannel.
- An interface that is already configured to be a Switched Port Analyzer (SPAN) destination port will not join an EtherChannel group until SPAN is disabled.
- Do not configure a secure port as part of an EtherChannel.
- Interfaces with different native VLANs cannot form an EtherChannel.
- When using trunk links, ensure that all trunks are in the same mode—Inter-Switch Link (ISL) or Dot1Q.

Configuring L2 EtherChannel

Switch(config)#**interface range fastethernet 0/1 - 4**	Moves to interface range config mode.
Switch(config-if-range)#**channel-protocol pagp**	Specifies the PAgP protocol to be used in this channel.
or	
Switch(config-if-range)#**channel-protocol lacp**	Specifies the LACP protocol to be used in this channel.
Switch(config-if-range)#**channel-group 1 mode {desirable I auto I on I passive I active }**	Creates channel group 1 and assigns interfaces 01–04 as part of it. Use whichever mode is necessary, depending on your choice of protocol.
Switch(config)#**interface port-channel {number}** Switch(config-if)# **Interface parameters**	Specifies the port-channel interface. Once in the interface configuration mode, you can configure additional parameters.

Configuring L3 EtherChannel

3560Switch(config)#**interface port-channel 1**	Creates the port-channel logical interface and moves to interface config mode. Valid channel numbers are 1–48.
3560Switch(config-if)#**no switchport**	Puts the interface into Layer 3 mode.
3560Switch(config-if)#**ip address 172.16.10.1 255.255.255.0**	Assigns IP address and netmask.
3560Switch(config-if)#**exit**	Moves to global config mode.
3560Switch(config)#**interface range fastethernet 0/20 - 24**	Moves to interface range config mode.
3560Switch(config-if-range)#**no ip address**	Ensures there are no IP addresses assigned on the interfaces.
3560Switch(config-if-range)#**channel-protocol pagp**	Specifies the PAgP protocol to be used in this channel.
3560Switch(config-if-range)#**channel-protocol lacp**	Specifies the LACP protocol to be used in this channel.
	NOTE: Either PAgP or LACP can be used as the port aggregation protocol.
3560Switch(config-if-range)#**channel-group 1 mode {desirable | auto | on | passive | active }**	Creates channel group 1 and assigns interfaces 20–24 as part of it. Use whichever mode is necessary, depending on your choice of protocol.
	NOTE: The channel group number must match the port channel number.

Verifying EtherChannel

Switch#**show running-config**	Displays list of what is currently running on the device.
Switch#**show running-config interface fastethernet 0/12**	Displays interface fastethernet 0/12 information.
Switch#**show interfaces fastethernet 0/12 etherchannel**	Displays interface EtherChannel information.

Switch#`show etherchannel`	Displays all EtherChannel information.
Switch#`show etherchannel 1 port-channel`	Displays port channel information.
Switch#`show etherchannel summary`	Displays a summary of EtherChannel information.
Switch#`show pagp neighbor`	Shows PAgP neighbor information.
Switch#`clear pagp 1 counters`	Clears PAgP channel group 1 information.
Switch#`clear lacp 1 counters`	Clears LACP channel group 1 information.
Switch(config)#`port-channel load-balance` *type*	Configures load balancing of method named *type*.
	NOTE: The following methods are allowed when load balancing across a port channel:
	dst-ip—Distribution is based on destination host IP address.
	dst-mac—Distribution is based on the destination MAC address. Packets to the same destination are sent on the same port, but packets to different destinations are sent on different ports in the channel.
	src-dst-ip—Distribution is based on source and destination host IP address.
	src-dst-mac—Distribution is based on source and destination MAC address.
	src-ip—Distribution is based on source IP address.
	src-mac—Distribution is based on source MAC address. Packets from different hosts use different ports in the channel, but packets from the same host use the same port.
Switch#`show etherchannel load-balance`	Displays EtherChannel load-balancing information.

Configuration Example: EtherChannel

Figure 2-3 shows the network topology for the configuration that follows, which shows how to configure EtherChannel using commands covered in this chapter.

Figure 2-3   Network Topology for EtherChannel Configuration

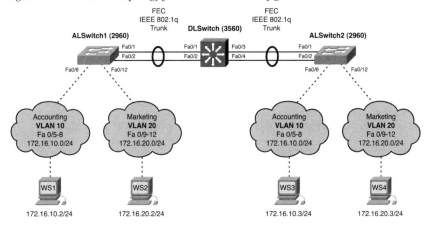

DLSwitch (3560)

Switch>**enable**	Moves to privileged mode.
Switch#**configure terminal**	Moves to global config mode.
Switch(config)#**hostname DLSwitch**	Sets host name.
DLSwitch(config)#**no ip domain-lookup**	Turns off DNS queries so that spelling mistakes will not slow you down.
DLSwitch(config)#**vtp mode server**	Changes the switch to VTP server mode.
DLSwitch(config)#**vtp domain testdomain**	Configures the VTP domain name to testdomain.
DLSwitch(config)#**vlan 10**	Creates VLAN 10 and enters VLAN-config mode.
DLSwitch(config-vlan)#**name Accounting**	Assigns a name to the VLAN.
DLSwitch(config-vlan)#**exit**	Returns to global config mode.
DLSwitch(config)#**vlan 20**	Creates VLAN 20 and enters VLAN-config mode.

DLSwitch(config-vlan)#**name Marketing**	Assigns a name to the VLAN.
DLSwitch(config-vlan)#**exit**	Returns to global config mode.
DLSwitch(config)#**interface range fastethernet 0/1 - 4**	Moves to interface range config mode.
DLSwitch(config-if)#**switchport trunk encapsulation dot1q**	Specifies 802.1Q encapsulation on the trunk link.
DLSwitch(config-if)#**switchport mode trunk**	Puts the interface into permanent trunking mode and negotiates to convert the link into a trunk link.
DLSwitch(config-if)#**exit**	Returns to global config mode.
DLSwitch(config)#**interface range fastethernet 0/1 - 2**	Moves to interface range config mode.
DLSwitch(config-if)#**channel-group 1 mode desirable**	Creates channel group 1 and assigns interfaces 0/1–0/2 as part of it.
DLSwitch(config-if)#**exit**	Moves to global config mode.
DLSwitch(config)#**interface range fastethernet 0/3 - 4**	Moves to interface range config mode.
DLSwitch(config-if)#**channel-group 2 mode desirable**	Creates channel group 2 and assigns interfaces 0/3–0/4 as part of it.
DLSwitch(config-if)#**exit**	Moves to global config mode.
DLSwitch(config)#**port-channel load-balance dst-mac**	Configures load balancing based on destination MAC address.
DLSwitch(config)#**exit**	Moves to privileged mode.
DLSwitch#**copy running-config startup-config**	Saves the configuration to NVRAM.

ALSwitch1 (2960)

Switch>**enable**	Moves to privileged mode.
Switch#**configure terminal**	Moves to global config mode.
Switch(config)#**hostname ALSwitch1**	Sets the host name.
ALSwitch1(config)#**no ip domain-lookup**	Turns off DNS queries so that spelling mistakes will not slow you down.

ALSwitch1(config)#**vtp mode client**	Changes the switch to VTP client mode.
ALSwitch1(config)#**vtp domain testdomain**	Configures the VTP domain name to testdomain.
ALSwitch1(config)#**interface range fastethernet 0/5 - 8**	Moves to interface range config mode.
ALSwitch1(config-if-range)#**switchport mode access**	Sets ports 5–8 as access ports.
ALSwitch1(config-if-range)#**switchport access vlan 10**	Assigns ports to VLAN 10.
ALSwitch1(config-if-range)#**exit**	Moves to global config mode.
ALSwitch1(config)#**interface range fastethernet 0/9 – 12**	Moves to interface range config mode.
ALSwitch1(config-if-range)#**switchport mode access**	Sets ports 9–12 as access ports.
ALSwitch1(config-if-range)#**switchport access vlan 20**	Assigns ports to VLAN 20.
ALSwitch1(config-if-range)#**exit**	Moves to global config mode.
ALSwitch1(config)#**interface range fastethernet 0/1 - 2**	Moves to interface range config mode.
ALSwitch1(config-if-range)#**switchport mode trunk**	Puts the interface into permanent trunking mode and negotiates to convert the link into a trunk link.
ALSwitch1(config-if-range)#**channel-group 1 mode desirable**	Creates channel group 1 and assigns interfaces 0/1–0/2 as part of it.
ALSwitch1(config-if-range)#**exit**	Moves to global config mode.
ALSwitch1(config)#**exit**	Moves to privileged mode.
ALSwitch1#**copy running-config startup-config**	Saves the configuration to NVRAM.

ALSwitch2 (2960)

Switch>**enable**	Moves to privileged mode.
Switch#**configure terminal**	Moves to global config mode.

`Switch(config)#`**`hostname ALSwitch2`**	Sets the host name.
`ALSwitch2(config)#`**`no ip domain-`** **`lookup`**	Turns off DNS queries so that spelling mistakes will not slow you down.
`ALSwitch2(config)#`**`vtp mode client`**	Changes the switch to VTP client mode.
`ALSwitch2(config)#`**`vtp domain`** **`testdomain`**	Configures the VTP domain name to testdomain.
`ALSwitch2(config)#`**`interface range`** **`fastethernet 0/5 - 8`**	Moves to interface range config mode.
`ALSwitch2(config-if-` `range)#`**`switchport mode access`**	Sets ports 5–8 as access ports.
`ALSwitch2(config-if-` `range)#`**`switchport access vlan 10`**	Assigns ports to VLAN 10.
`ALSwitch2(config-if-range)#`**`exit`**	Moves to global config mode.
`ALSwitch2(config)#`**`interface range`** **`fastethernet 0/9 - 12`**	Moves to interface range config mode.
`ALSwitch2(config-if-` `range)#`**`switchport mode access`**	Sets ports 9–12 as access ports.
`ALSwitch2(config-if-` `range)#`**`switchport access vlan 20`**	Assigns ports to VLAN 20.
`ALSwitch2(config-if-range)#`**`exit`**	Moves to global config mode.
`ALSwitch2(config)#`**`interface range`** **`fastethernet 0/1 - 2`**	Moves to interface range config mode.
`ALSwitch2(config-if-` `range)#`**`switchport mode trunk`**	Puts the interface into permanent trunking mode and negotiates to convert the link into a trunk link.
`ALSwitch2(config-if-range)#`**`channel-`** **`group 1 mode desirable`**	Creates channel group 1 and assigns interfaces 0/1–0/2 as part of it.
`ALSwitch2(config-if-range)#`**`exit`**	Moves to global config mode.
`ALSwitch2(config)#`**`exit`**	Moves to privileged mode.
`ALSwitch2#`**`copy running-config`** **`startup-config`**	Saves the configuration to NVRAM.

CHAPTER 3

Implementing Spanning Tree

This chapter provides information and commands concerning the following topics:

- Enabling Spanning Tree Protocol
- Configuring the root switch
- Configuring a secondary root switch
- Configuring port priority
- Configuring the path cost
- Configuring the switch priority of a VLAN
- Configuring STP timers
- Verifying STP
- Optional STP configurations
  - PortFast
  - BPDU Guard
  - BPDU Filtering
  - UplinkFast
  - BackboneFast
  - Root Guard
  - Loop Guard
  - Unidirectional Link Detection
- Changing the spanning-tree mode
- Extended System ID
- Enabling Rapid Spanning Tree
- Enabling Multiple Spanning Tree
- Verifying MST
- Troubleshooting STP

Enabling Spanning Tree Protocol

`Switch(config)#spanning-tree vlan 5`	Enables Spanning Tree Protocol (STP) on VLAN 5.
`Switch(config)#no spanning-tree vlan 5`	Disables STP on VLAN 5.

NOTE: If more VLANs are defined in the VLAN Trunking Protocol (VTP) than there are spanning-tree instances, you can have only STP on 64 VLANs. If you have more than 128 VLANs, it is recommended that you use Multiple STP.

Configuring the Root Switch

`Switch(config)#`**`spanning-tree`** **`vlan 5 root`**	Modifies the switch priority from the default 32768 to a lower value to enable the switch to become the root switch for VLAN 5.
	NOTE: If all other switches have extended system ID support, this switch resets its priority to 24576. If any other switch has a priority set to below 24576 already, this switch sets its own priority to 4096 *less* than the lowest switch priority. If by doing this the switch would have a priority of less than 1, this command fails.
`Switch(config)#`**`spanning-tree`** **`vlan 5 root primary`**	Switch recalculates timers along with priority to enable the switch to become the root switch for VLAN 5.
	TIP: The root switch should be a backbone or distribution switch.
`Switch(config)#`**`spanning-tree`** **`vlan 5 root primary diameter 7`**	Configures the switch to be the root switch for VLAN 5 and sets the network diameter to 7.
	TIP: The **diameter** keyword defines the maximum number of switches between any two end stations. The range is from 2 to 7 switches.
`Switch(config)#`**`spanning-tree`** **`vlan 5 root primary hello-time 4`**	Configures the switch to be the root switch for VLAN 5 and sets the hello-delay timer to 4 seconds.
	TIP: The **hello-time** keyword sets the hello-delay timer to any amount between 1 and 10 seconds. The default time is 2 seconds.

Configuring a Secondary Root Switch

`Switch(config)#`**`spanning-tree`** **`vlan 5 root secondary`**	Switch recalculates timers along with priority to enable the switch to become the root switch for VLAN 5 if the primary root switch fails.
	NOTE: If all other switches have extended system ID support, this switch resets its priority to 28672. Therefore, if the root switch fails, and all other switches are set to the default priority of 32768, this becomes the new root switch. For switches without Extended System ID support, the switch priority is changed to 16384.
`Switch(config)#`**`spanning-tree`** **`vlan 5 root secondary diameter 7`**	Configures the switch to be the secondary root switch for VLAN 5 and sets the network diameter to 7.
`Switch(config)#`**`spanning-tree vlan`** **`5 root secondary hello-time 4`**	Configures the switch to be the secondary root switch for VLAN 5 and sets the hello-delay timer to 4 seconds.

Configuring Port Priority

`Switch(config)#`**`interface`** **`gigabitethernet 0/1`**	Moves to interface configuration mode.
`Switch(config-if)#`**`spanning-tree`** **`port-priority 64`**	Configures the port priority for the interface that is an access port.
`Switch(config-if)#`**`spanning-tree`** **`vlan 5 port-priority 64`**	Configures the VLAN port priority for an interface that is a trunk port.
	NOTE: Port priority is used to break a tie when two switches have equal priorities for determining the root switch. The number can be between 0 and 255. The default port priority is 128. The lower the number, the higher the priority.

Configuring the Path Cost

`Switch(config)#interface gigabitethernet 0/1`	Moves to interface config mode.
`Switch(config-if)#spanning-tree cost 100000`	Configures the cost for the interface that is an access port.
`Switch(config-if)#spanning-tree vlan 5 cost 1000000`	Configures the VLAN cost for an interface that is a trunk port.
	NOTE: If a loop occurs, STP uses the path cost when trying to determine which interface to place into the forwarding state. A higher path cost means a lower speed transmission. The range of the **cost** keyword is 1 through 200000000. The default is based on the media speed of the interface.

Configuring the Switch Priority of a VLAN

`Switch(config)#spanning-tree vlan 5 priority 12288`	Configures the switch priority of VLAN 5 to 12288.

NOTE: With the **priority** keyword, the range is 0 to 61440 in increments of 4096. The default is 32768. The lower the priority, the more likely the switch will be chosen as the root switch.

Only the following numbers can be used as a priority value:

0	4096	8192	12288
16384	20480	24576	28672
32768	36864	40960	45056
49152	53248	57344	61440

CAUTION: Cisco recommends caution when using this command. Cisco further recommends that the **spanning-tree vlan** *x* **root primary** or the **spanning-tree vlan** *x* **root secondary** command be used instead to modify the switch priority.

Configuring STP Timers

Switch(config)#**spanning-tree vlan 5 hello-time 4**	Changes the hello-delay timer to 4 seconds on VLAN 5.
Switch(config)#**spanning-tree vlan 5 forward-time 20**	Changes the forward-delay timer to 20 seconds on VLAN 5.
Switch(config)#**spanning-tree vlan 5 max-age 25**	Changes the maximum-aging timer to 25 seconds on VLAN 5.

NOTE: For the **hello-time** command, the range is 1 to 10 seconds. The default is 2 seconds.

NOTE: For the **forward-time** command, the range is 4 to 30 seconds. The default is 15 seconds.

For the **max-age** command, the range is 6 to 40 seconds. The default is 20 seconds.

CAUTION: Cisco recommends caution when using this command. Cisco further recommends that the **spanning-tree vlan** *x* **root primary** or the **spanning-tree vlan** *x* **root secondary** command be used instead to modify the switch timers.

FlexLinks

Switch(config)#**interface fastethernet1/0/1**	Moves to interface configuration mode.
Switch(config-if)#**switchport backup interface fastethernet1/0/2**	Configures FastEthernet 1/0/2 to provide Layer 2 backup to FastEthernet 1/0/1.
Switch#**show interface switchport backup**	Shows all the Layer 2 switch backup interface pairs.
	NOTE: FlexLink is an alternative solution to the Spanning Tree Protocol.

Verifying STP

Switch#**show spanning-tree**	Displays STP information.
Switch#**show spanning-tree active**	Displays STP information on active interfaces only.
Switch#**show spanning-tree brief**	Displays a brief status of the STP.
Switch#**show spanning-tree detail**	Displays a detailed summary of interface information.
Switch#**show spanning-tree interface gigabitethernet 0/1**	Displays STP information for interface gigabitethernet 0/1.
Switch#**show spanning-tree summary**	Displays a summary of port states.
Switch#**show spanning-tree summary totals**	Displays the total lines of the STP section.
Switch#**show spanning-tree vlan 5**	Displays STP information for VLAN 5.

Optional STP Configurations

Although the following commands are not mandatory for STP to work, you might find these helpful in fine-tuning your network.

PortFast

Switch(config)#**interface fastethernet 0/10**	Moves to interface config mode.
Switch(config-if)#**spanning-tree portfast**	Enables PortFast on an access port.
Switch(config-if)#**spanning-tree portfast trunk**	Enables PortFast on a trunk port.
	CAUTION: Use the **portfast** command only when connecting a single end station to an access or trunk port. Using this command on a port connected to a switch or hub could prevent spanning tree from detecting loops.

	NOTE: If you enable the voice VLAN feature, PortFast is enabled automatically. If you disable voice VLAN, PortFast is still enabled.
Switch#**show spanning-tree interface fastethernet 0/10 portfast**	Displays PortFast information on interface fastethernet 0/10.

BPDU Guard

Switch(config)#**spanning-tree portfast bpduguard default**	Globally enables BPDU Guard.
Switch(config)#**interface range fastethernet 0/1 - 5**	Enters interface range configuration mode.
Switch(config-if-range)#**spanning-tree portfast**	Enables PortFast on all interfaces in the range.
	NOTE: By default, BPDU Guard is disabled.
Switch(config)#**errdisable recovery cause bpduguard**	Enables the port to reenable itself if the cause of the error is BPDU Guard by setting a recovery timer.
Switch(config)#**errdisable recovery interval 400**	Sets the recovery timer to 400 seconds. The default is 300 seconds. Range is from 30 to 86400 seconds.
Switch#**show spanning-tree summary totals**	Verifies whether BPDU Guard is enabled or disabled.
Switch#**show errdisable recovery**	Displays errdisable recovery timer information.

BPDU Filtering

Switch(config)#**spanning-tree portfast bpdufilter default**	Globally enables BPDU Filtering—prevents ports in PortFast from sending or receiving bridge protocol data units (BPDU).
Switch(config)#**interface range fastethernet 0/1 - 5**	Enters interface range configuration mode.

`Switch(config-if-range)#spanning-tree portfast`	Enables PortFast on all interfaces in the range.
	NOTE: By default, BPDU Filtering is disabled.
	CAUTION: Enabling BPDU Filtering on an interface, or globally, is the same as disabling STP, which can result in spanning-tree loops being created but not detected.
`Switch(config)#interface fastethernet 0/15`	Enters interface configuration mode.
`Switch(config-if)#spanning-tree bpdufilter enable`	Enables BPDU Filtering on the interface without enabling the PortFast feature.
`Switch#show spanning-tree summary totals`	Displays Global BPDU Filtering configuration information.
`Switch#show running-config`	Verifies BPDU Filtering is enabled on interfaces.

UplinkFast

`Switch(config)#spanning-tree uplinkfast`	Enables UplinkFast.
`Switch(config)#spanning-tree uplinkfast max-update-rate 200`	Enables UplinkFast and sets the update packet rate to 200 packets/second.
	NOTE: UplinkFast cannot be set on an individual VLAN. The **spanning-tree uplinkfast** command affects all VLANs.
	NOTE: For the **max-update-rate** argument, the range is 0 to 32000 packets/second. The default is 150. If you set the rate to 0, station-learning frames are not generated. This causes STP to converge more slowly after a loss of connectivity.
`Switch#show spanning-tree summary`	Verifies whether UplinkFast has been enabled.

NOTE: UplinkFast cannot be enabled on VLANs that have been configured for switch priority.

NOTE: UplinkFast is most useful in access-layer switches, or switches at the edge of the network. It is not appropriate for backbone devices.

BackboneFast

`Switch(config)#`**`spanning-tree backbonefast`**	Enables BackboneFast.
`Switch#`**`show spanning-tree summary`**	Verifies whether BackboneFast has been enabled.

Root Guard

`Switch(config)#`**`interface fastethernet 0/1`**	Enters interface configuration mode.
`Switch(config-if)#`**`spanning-tree guard root`**	Enables Root Guard on the interface.
`Switch#`**`show spanning-tree inconsistentports`**	Indicates whether any ports are in a rootinconsistent state.
`Switch#`**`show running-config`**	Verifies whether Root Guard is enabled on the interface.

NOTE: You cannot enable both Root Guard and Loop Guard at the same time.

NOTE: Root Guard enabled on an interface applies to all VLANs to which the interface belongs.

NOTE: Do not enable Root Guard on interfaces to be used by the UplinkFast feature.

Loop Guard

`Switch#`**`show spanning-tree active`**	Shows which ports are alternate or root ports.
`Switch#`**`show spanning-tree mst`**	Shows which ports are alternate or root ports.

Switch#**configure terminal**	Enters global configuration mode.
Switch(config)#**spanning-tree loopguard default**	Enables Loop Guard globally on the switch.
Switch(config)#**exit**	Returns to privileged mode.
Switch#**show running-config**	Verifies that Loop Guard has been enabled.

NOTE: You cannot enable both Root Guard and Loop Guard at the same time.

NOTE: This feature is most effective when it is configured on the entire switched network.

NOTE: Loop Guard operates only on ports that are considered to be point to point by the STP.

Unidirectional Link Detection

Switch(config)#**udld enable**	Enables Unidirectional Link Detection (UDLD) on all fiber-optic interfaces.
	NOTE: By default, UDLD is disabled.
Switch(config)#**udld aggressive**	Enables Unidirectional Link Detection aggressive mode (UDLD) on all fiber-optic and twisted pair interfaces.
Switch(config)#**interface fastethernet 0/24**	Moves to interface config mode.
Switch(config-if)#**udld port**	Enables UDLD on this interface—required for copper-based interfaces.
	NOTE: On a fiber-optic interface, the interface command **udld port** overrides the global command **udld enable**. Therefore, if you issue the command **no udld port** on an interface, you still have to deal with the globally enabled **udld enable** command.
Switch#**show udld**	Displays UDLD information.
Switch#**show udld fastethernet 0/1**	Displays UDLD information for interface fastethernet 0/1.

Switch#**udld reset**	Resets all interfaces shut down by UDLD.
	NOTE: You can also use the **shutdown** command, followed by a **no shutdown** command in interface config mode, to restart a disabled interface.

Changing the Spanning-Tree Mode

Different types of spanning tree can be configured on a Cisco switch. The options vary according to the platform:

- **Per-VLAN Spanning Tree (PVST)**—There is one instance of spanning tree for each VLAN. This is a Cisco proprietary protocol.
- **Per-VLAN Spanning Tree Plus (PVST+)**—This Cisco proprietary has added extensions to the PVST protocol.
- **Rapid PVST+**—This mode is the same as PVST+ except that it uses a rapid convergence based on the 802.1w standard.
- **Multiple Spanning Tree Protocol (MSTP)**—IEEE 802.1s. Extends the 802.1w Rapid Spanning Tree (RST) algorithm to multiple spanning trees. Multiple VLANs can map to a single instance of RST. You cannot run MSTP and PVST at the same time.

Switch(config)#**spanning-tree mode mst**	Enables MSTP. This command is available only on a switch running the Enhanced Image (EI) software image.
Switch(config)#**spanning-tree mode pvst**	Enables PVST—this is the default setting.
Switch(config)#**spanning-tree mode rapid-pvst**	Enables Rapid PVST+.

Extended System ID

Switch(config)#**spanning-tree extend system-id**	Enables Extended System ID, also known as MAC Address Reduction.
	NOTE: Catalyst switches running software earlier than Cisco IOS Release 12.1(8)EA1 do not support the Extended System ID.

Switch#**show spanning-tree summary**	Display a summary of port states, statistics, and enabled features.
Switch#**show running-config**	Display the current volatile device configuration.

Enabling Rapid Spanning Tree

Switch(config)#**spanning-tree mode rapid-pvst**	Enables Rapid PVST+.
Switch(config)#**interface fastethernet 0/1**	Moves to interface config mode.
Switch(config-if)#**spanning-tree link-type point-to-point**	Sets the interface to be a point-to-point interface.
	NOTE: By setting the link type to point-to-point, this means that if you connect this port to a remote port, and this port becomes a designated port, the switch will negotiate with the remote port and transition the local port to a forwarding state.
Switch(config-if)#**exit**	
Switch(config)#**clear spanning-tree detected-protocols**	
	NOTE: The **clear spanning-tree detected-protocols** command restarts the protocol migration process on the switch if any port is connected to a port on a legacy 802.1D switch.

Enabling Multiple Spanning Tree

Switch(config)#**spanning-tree mst configuration**	Enters MST configuration mode.
Switch(config-mst)#**instance 1 vlan 4**	Maps VLAN 4 to a Multiple Spanning Tree (MST) instance.

`Switch(config-mst)#`**`instance 1 vlan 1-15`**	Maps VLANs 1–15 to MST instance 1.
`Switch(config-mst)#`**`instance 1 vlan 10,20,30`**	Maps VLANs 10, 20, and 30 to MST instance 1.
	NOTE: For the **instance** *x* **vlan** *y* command, the instance must be a number between 1 and 15 and the VLAN range is 1 to 4094.
`Switch(config-mst)#`**`name region12`**	Specifies the configuration name to be region12.
	NOTE: The **name** argument can be up to 32 characters long and is case sensitive.
`Switch(config-mst)#`**`revision 4`**	Specifies the revision number.
	NOTE: The range for the **revision** argument is 0 to 65535.
`Switch(config-mst)#`**`show pending`**	Verifies the configuration by displaying a summary of what you have configured for the MST region.
`Switch(config-mst)#`**`exit`**	Applies all changes and returns to global configuration mode.
`Switch(config)#`**`spanning-tree mst 1`**	Enables MST.
	CAUTION: Changing spanning-tree modes can disrupt traffic because all spanning-tree instances are stopped for the old mode and restarted in the new mode.
	NOTE: You cannot run both MSTP and PVST at the same time.
`Switch(config)#`**`spanning-tree mst 1 root primary`**	Configures a switch as a primary root switch within MST instance 1. The primary root switch priority is 24576.

Switch(config)#**spanning-tree mst 1 root secondary**	Configures a switch as a secondary root switch within MST instance 1. The secondary root switch priority is 28672.
Switch(config)#**exit**	Returns to privileged mode.

Verifying MST

Switch#**show spanning-tree mst configuration**	Displays the MST region configuration.
Switch#**show spanning-tree mst 1**	Displays the MST information for instance 1.
Switch#**show spanning-tree mst interface fastethernet 0/1**	Displays the MST information for interface fastethernet 0/1.
Switch#**show spanning-tree mst 1 interface fastethernet 0/1**	Displays the MST information for instance 1 on interface fastethernet 0/1.
Switch#**show spanning-tree mst 1 detail**	Shows detailed information about MST instance 1.

Troubleshooting Spanning Tree

Switch#**debug spanning-tree all**	Displays all spanning-tree debugging events.
Switch#**debug spanning-tree events**	Displays spanning-tree debugging topology events.
Switch#**debug spanning-tree backbonefast**	Displays spanning-tree debugging BackboneFast events.
Switch#**debug spanning-tree uplinkfast**	Displays spanning-tree debugging UplinkFast event.
Switch#**debug spanning-tree mstp all**	Displays all MST debugging events.
Switch#**debug spanning-tree switch state**	Displays spanning-tree port state changes.
Switch#**debug spanning-tree pvst+**	Displays PVST+ events.

Configuration Example: STP

Figure 3-1 shows the network topology for the configuration that follows, which shows how to configure STP using commands covered in this chapter.

Figure 3-1   Network Topology for STP Configuration Example

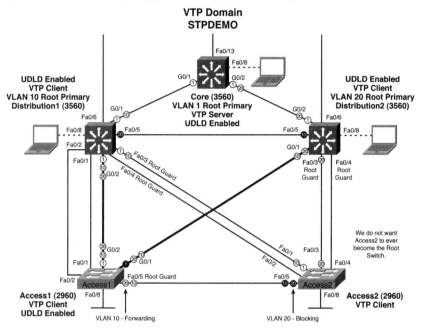

Core Switch (3560)

Switch>**enable**	Moves to privileged mode.
Switch#**configure terminal**	Moves to global config mode.
Switch(config)#**hostname Core**	Sets the host name.
Core(config)#**no ip domain-lookup**	Turns off Dynamic Name System (DNS) queries so that spelling mistakes will not slow you down.
Core(config)#**vtp mode server**	Changes the switch to VTP server mode. This is the default mode.
Core(config)#**vtp domain stpdemo**	Configures the VTP domain name to stpdemo.

Core(config)#**vlan 10**	Creates VLAN 10 and enters VLAN-config mode.
Core(config-vlan)#**name Accounting**	Assigns a name to the VLAN.
Core(config-vlan)#**exit**	Returns to global config mode.
Core(config)#**vlan 20**	Creates VLAN 20 and enters VLAN-config mode.
Core(config-vlan)#**name Marketing**	Assigns a name to the VLAN.
Core(config-vlan)#**exit**	Returns to global config mode.
Core(config)#**spanning-tree vlan 1 root primary**	Configures the switch to become the root switch for VLAN 1.
Core(config)#**udld enable**	Enables UDLD.
Core(config)#**exit**	Returns to privileged mode.
Core#**copy running-config startup-config**	Saves the configuration to Non-Volatile RAM (NVRAM).

Distribution 1 Switch (3560)

Switch>**enable**	Moves to privileged mode.
Switch#**configure terminal**	Moves to global configuration mode.
Switch(config)#**hostname Distribution1**	Sets the host name.
Distribution1(config)#**no ip domain-lookup**	Turns off DNS queries so that spelling mistakes will not slow you down.
Distribution1(config)#**vtp domain stpdemo**	Configures the VTP domain name to stpdemo.
Distribution1(config)#**vtp mode client**	Changes the switch to VTP client mode.
Distribution1(config)#**spanning-tree vlan 10 root primary**	Configures the switch to become the root switch of VLAN 10.
Distribution1(config)#**udld enable**	Enables UDLD on all FO interfaces.
Distribution1(config)#**interface range fastethernet 0/3 - 4**	Enters interface range mode.

`Distribution1(config-if)#spanning-` `tree guard root`	Prevents switch on the other end of the link (Access2) from becoming the root switch.
`Distribution1(config-if)#exit`	Returns to global configuration mode.
`Distribution1(config)#exit`	Returns to privileged mode.
`Distribution1#copy running-config` `startup-config`	Saves the configuration to NVRAM.

Distribution 2 Switch (3560)

`Switch>enable`	Moves to privileged mode.
`Switch#configure terminal`	Moves to global configuration mode.
`Switch(config)#hostname` `Distribution2`	Sets the host name.
`Distribution2(config)#no ip domain-` `lookup`	Turns off DNS queries so that spelling mistakes will not slow you down.
`Distribution2(config)#vtp domain` `stpdemo`	Configures the VTP domain name to stpdemo.
`Distribution2(config)#vtp mode` `client`	Changes the switch to VTP client mode.
`Distribution2(config)#spanning-tree` `vlan 20 root primary`	Configures the switch to become the root switch of VLAN 20.
`Distribution2(config)#udld enable`	Enables UDLD on all FO interfaces.
`Distribution2(config)#interface` `range fastethernet 0/3 - 4`	Moves to interface range mode.
`Distribution2(config-if)#spanning-` `tree guard root`	Prevents the switch on the other end of link (Access2) from becoming the root switch.
`Distribution2(config-if)#exit`	Returns to global config mode.
`Distribution2(config)#exit`	Returns to privileged mode.
`Distribution2#copy running-config` `startup-config`	Saves the configuration to NVRAM.

Access 1 Switch (2960)

`Switch>enable`	Moves to privileged mode.
`Switch#configure terminal`	Moves to global configuration mode.
`Switch(config)#hostname Access1`	Sets the host name.
`Access1(config)#no ip domain-lookup`	Turns off DNS queries so that spelling mistakes will not slow you down.
`Access1(config)#vtp domain stpdemo`	Configures the VTP domain name to stpdemo.
`Access1(config)#vtp mode client`	Changes the switch to VTP client mode.
`Access1(config)#interface range fastethernet 0/6 - 12`	Moves to interface range configuration mode.
`Access1(config-if-range)#switchport mode access`	Places all interfaces in access mode.
`Access1(config-if-range)#spanning-tree portfast`	Places all ports directly into forwarding mode.
`Access1(config-if-range)#spanning-tree bpduguard enable`	Enables BPDU Guard.
`Access1(config-if-range)#exit`	Moves back to global config mode.
`Access1(config)#spanning-tree uplinkfast`	Enables UplinkFast to reduce STP convergence time.
`Access1(config)#interface fastethernet 0/5`	Moves to interface config mode.
`Access1(config-if)#spanning-tree guard root`	Prevents the switch on the other end of link (Access2) from becoming the root switch.
`Access1(config-if)#exit`	Returns to global configuration mode.
`Access1(config)#udld enable`	Enables UDLD on all FO interfaces.
`Access1(config)#exit`	Returns to privileged mode.
`Access1#copy running-config startup-config`	Saves the configuration to NVRAM.

Access 2 Switch (2960)

`Switch>`**`enable`**	Moves to privileged mode.
`Switch#`**`configure terminal`**	Moves to global configuration mode.
`Switch(config)#`**`hostname Access2`**	Sets host name.
`Access2(config)#`**`no ip domain-lookup`**	Turns off DNS queries so that spelling mistakes will not slow you down.
`Access2(config)#`**`vtp domain stpdemo`**	Configures the VTP domain name to stpdemo.
`Access2(config)#`**`vtp mode client`**	Changes the switch to VTP client mode.
`Access2(config)#`**`interface range fastethernet 0/6 - 12`**	Moves to interface range configuration mode.
`Access2(config-if-range)#`**`switchport mode access`**	Places all interfaces in access mode.
`Access2(config-if-range)#`**`spanning- tree portfast`**	Places all ports directly into forwarding mode.
`Access2(config-if-range)#`**`spanning- tree bpduguard enable`**	Enables BPDU Guard.
`Access2(config-if-range)#`**`exit`**	Returns to global configuration mode.
`Access2(config)#`**`exit`**	Returns to privileged mode.
`Access2#`**`copy running-config startup-config`**	Saves config to NVRAM.

CHAPTER 4

Implementing Inter-VLAN Routing

This chapter provides information and commands concerning the following topics:

Inter-VLAN communication

- Inter-VLAN communication using an external router: router-on-a-stick
- Inter-VLAN communication tips
- Inter-VLAN communication on a multilayer switch through a switch virtual interface
  - Removing L2 switchport capability of a switch port
  - Configuring SVI Autostate
  - Configuring a Layer 3 EtherChannel
  - Configuring inter-VLAN communication
- Configuration example: inter-VLAN communication

DHCP

- Configuring DHCP server on a Router or Layer 3 Switch
- Verifying and troubleshooting DHCP configuration
- Configuring a DHCP helper address
- DHCP client on a Cisco IOS Software Ethernet interface
- Configuration example: DHCP

CEF

- Configuring Cisco Express Forwarding (CEF)
- Verifying CEF
- Troubleshooting CEF

Inter-VLAN Communication Using an External Router: Router-on-a-Stick

`Router(config)#interface fastethernet 0/0`	Moves to interface configuration mode.
`Router(config-if)#duplex full`	Sets interface to full duplex.
`Router(config-if)#no shutdown`	Enables interface.
`Router(config-if)#interface fastethernet 0/0.1`	Creates subinterface 0/0.1 and moves to subinterface configuration mode.

`Router(config-subif)#`**`description`** **`Management VLAN 1`**	(Optional) Sets locally significant descriptor of the subinterface.
`Router(config-subif)#`**`encapsulation`** **`dot1q 1 native`**	Assigns VLAN 1 to this subinterface. VLAN 1 is the native VLAN. This subinterface uses the 802.1Q trunking protocol.
`Router(config-subif)#`**`ip address`** **`192.168.1.1 255.255.255.0`**	Assigns IP address and netmask.
`Router(config-subif)#`**`interface`** **`fastethernet 0/0.10`**	Creates subinterface 0/0.10 and moves to subinterface configuration mode.
`Router(config-subif)#`**`description`** **`Accounting VLAN 10`**	(Optional) Sets locally significant descriptor of the subinterface.
`Router(config-subif)#`**`encapsulation`** **`dot1q 10`**	Assigns VLAN 10 to this subinterface. This subinterface uses the 802.1Q trunking protocol.
`Router(config-subif)#`**`ip address`** **`192.168.10.1 255.255.255.0`**	Assigns IP address and netmask.
`Router(config-subif)#`**`exit`**	Returns to interface configuration mode.
`Router(config-if)#`**`exit`**	Returns to global configuration mode.
`Router(config)#`	

NOTE: The subnets of the VLANs are directly connected to the router. Routing between these subnets does not require a dynamic routing protocol. In a more complex topology, these routes need to either be advertised with whatever dynamic routing protocol is used, or be redistributed into whatever dynamic routing protocol is used.

NOTE: Routes to the subnets associated with these VLANs appear in the routing table as directly connected networks.

Inter-VLAN Communication Tips

- Although most routers support both Inter-Switch Link (ISL) and Dot1Q encapsulation, some switch models support only Dot1Q, such as the 2950 and 2960 series.
- If you need to use ISL as your trunking protocol, use the command **encapsulation isl** *x*, where *x* is the number of the VLAN to be assigned to that subinterface.

- Recommended best practice is to use the same number of the VLAN number for the subinterface number. It is easier to troubleshoot VLAN 10 on subinterface fastethernet0/0.10 than on fastethernet0/0.2.
- The native VLAN (usually VLAN 1) cannot be configured on a subinterface for Cisco IOS releases that are earlier than 12.1(3)T. Native VLAN IP addresses will, therefore, need to be configured on the physical interface. Other VLAN traffic will be configured on subinterfaces:

```
Router(config)#interface fastethernet 0/0
Router(config-if)#encapsulation dot1q 1 native
Router(config-if)#ip address 192.168.1.1 255.255.255.0
Router(config-if)#interface fastethernet 0/0.10
Router(config-subif)#encapsulation dot1q 10
Router(config-subif)#ip address 192.168.10.1 255.255.255.0
```

Inter-VLAN Communication on a Multilayer Switch Through a Switch Virtual Interface

Rather than using an external router to provide inter-VLAN communication, a multilayer switch can perform the same task through the use of a switched virtual interface (SVI).

Removing L2 Switchport Capability of a Switch Port

3750Switch(config)#**interface fastethernet 0/1**	Moves to interface configuration mode.
3750Switch(config-if)#**no switchport**	Creates a Layer 3 port on the switch.
	NOTE: The **no switchport** command can be used on physical ports only on a Layer 3–capable switch.

Configuring SVI Autostate

3750Switch(config)#**interface fastethernet 0/1**	Moves to interface configuration mode.
3750Switch(config-if)#**switchport auto-state exclude**	Excludes the access port/trunk in defining the status of an SVI as up or down.
	NOTE: This command is commonly used for ports that are used for monitoring, for example, so that a monitoring port does not cause the SVI to remain "up" when no other ports are active in the VLAN.

NOTE: For the SVI line state to be up, at least one port in the VLAN must be up and forwarding. The **switchport auto-state exclude** command excludes a port from the SVI interface line-state up-or-down calculation.

Configuring a Layer 3 EtherChannel

Switch(config)#**interface port-channel 1**	Creates a virtual Layer 2 interface.
Switch(config-if)#**no switchport**	Changes interface to Layer 3 to enable the use of the IP address command.
Switch(config-if)#**ip address 172.32.52.10 255.255.255.0**	Assigns an IP address to the Layer 3 port-channel interface.
Switch(config)#**interface range fastethernet 5/4 - 5**	Moves to interface range configuration mode.
Switch(config-if-range)#**no switchport**	Creates Layer 3 ports on a switch.
Switch(config-if-range)#**channel-protocol pagp**	Configures port aggregation protocol.
Switch(config-if-range)#**channel-group 1 mode desirable**	Assigns the physical interfaces in the range to the EtherChannel group.

Configuring Inter-VLAN Communication

3550Switch(config)#**interface vlan 1**	Creates a virtual interface for VLAN 1 and enters interface configuration mode.
3550Switch(config-if)#**ip address 172.16.1.1 255.255.255.0**	Assigns IP address and netmask.
3550Switch(config-if)#**no shutdown**	Enables the interface.
3550Switch(config)#**interface vlan 10**	Creates a virtual interface for VLAN 10 and enters interface configuration mode.
3550Switch(config-if)#**ip address 172.16.10.1 255.255.255.0**	Assigns IP address and netmask.
3550Switch(config-if)#**no shutdown**	Enables the interface.
3550Switch(config)#**interface vlan 20**	Creates a virtual interface for VLAN 20 and enters interface configuration mode.

3550Switch(config-if)#**ip address 172.16.20.1 255.255.255.0**	Assigns IP address and netmask.
3550Switch(config-if)#**no shutdown**	Enables the interface.
3550Switch(config-if)#**exit**	Returns to global configuration mode.
3550Switch(config)#**ip routing**	Enables routing on the switch.

Configuration Example: Inter-VLAN Communication

Figure 4-1 shows the network topology for the configuration that follows, which shows how to configure inter-VLAN communication using commands covered in this chapter. Some commands used in this configuration are from previous chapters.

Figure 4-1   Network Topology for Inter-VLAN Communication Configuration

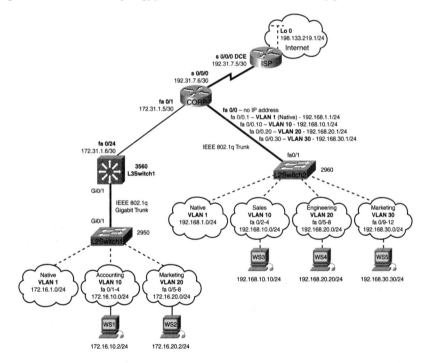

ISP Router

`Router>`**`enable`**	Moves to privileged mode.
`Router>#`**`configure terminal`**	Moves to global configuration mode.
`Router(config)#`**`hostname ISP`**	Sets the host name.
`ISP(config)#`**`interface loopback 0`**	Moves to interface configuration mode.
`ISP(config-if)#`**`description simulated address representing remote website`**	Sets the locally significant interface description.
`ISP(config-if)#`**`ip address 198.133.219.1 255.255.255.0`**	Assigns IP address and netmask.
`ISP(config-if)#`**`interface serial 0/0/0`**	Moves to interface configuration mode.
`ISP(config-if)#`**`description WAN link to the Corporate Router`**	Sets the locally significant interface description.
`ISP(config-if)#`**`ip address 192.31.7.5 255.255.255.252`**	Assigns IP address and netmask.
`ISP(config-if)#`**`clock rate 56000`**	Assigns a clock rate to the interface—DCE cable is plugged in to this interface.
`ISP(config-if)#`**`no shutdown`**	Enables the interface.
`ISP(config-if)#`**`exit`**	Returns to global configuration mode.
`ISP(config-if)#`**`router eigrp 10`**	Creates Enhanced Interior Gateway Routing Protocol (EIGRP) routing process 10.
`ISP(config-router)#`**`network 198.133.219.0`**	Advertises directly connected networks (classful address only).
`ISP(config-router)#`**`network 192.31.7.0`**	Advertises directly connected networks (classful address only).
`ISP(config-router)#`**`no auto-summary`**	Disables auto summarization.
`ISP(config-router)#`**`exit`**	Returns to global configuration mode.

`ISP(config)#`**`exit`**	Returns to privileged mode.
`ISP#`**`copy running-config startup-config`**	Saves the configuration to NVRAM.

CORP Router

`Router>`**`enable`**	Moves to privileged mode.
`Router>#`**`configure terminal`**	Moves to global configuration mode.
`Router(config)#`**`hostname CORP`**	Sets the host name.
`ISP(config)#`**`interface serial 0/0/0`**	Moves to interface configuration mode.
`CORP(config-if)#`**`description link to ISP`**	Sets the locally significant interface description.
`CORP(config-if)#`**`ip address 192.31.7.6 255.255.255.252`**	Assigns IP address and netmask.
`CORP(config-if)#`**`no shutdown`**	Enables the interface.
`CORP(config)#`**`interface fastethernet 0/1`**	Moves to interface configuration mode.
`CORP(config-if)#`**`description link to 3560 Switch`**	Sets the locally significant interface description.
`CORP(config-if)#`**`ip address 172.31.1.5 255.255.255.252`**	Assigns the IP address and netmask.
`CORP(config-if)#`**`no shutdown`**	Enables the interface.
`CORP(config-if)#`**`exit`**	Returns to global configuration mode.
`CORP(config)#`**`interface fastethernet 0/0`**	Enters interface configuration mode.
`CORP(config-if)#`**`duplex full`**	Enables full-duplex operation to ensure trunking will take effect between here and L2Switch2.
`CORP(config-if)#`**`no shutdown`**	Enables the interface.

`CORP(config-if)#interface fastethernet 0/0.1`	Creates a virtual subinterface and moves to subinterface configuration mode.
`CORP(config-subif)#description Management VLAN 1 - Native VLAN`	Sets the locally significant interface description.
`CORP(config-subif)#encapsulation dot1q 1 native`	Assigns VLAN 1 to this subinterface. VLAN 1 is the native VLAN. This subinterface uses the 802.1Q trunking protocol.
`CORP(config-subif)#ip address 192.168.1.1 255.255.255.0`	Assigns the IP address and netmask.
`CORP(config-subif)#interface fastethernet 0/0.10`	Creates a virtual subinterface and moves to subinterface configuration mode.
`CORP(config-subif)#description Sales VLAN 10`	Sets the locally significant interface description.
`CORP(config-subif)#encapsulation dot1q 10`	Assigns VLAN 10 to this subinterface. This subinterface uses the 802.1Q trunking protocol.
`CORP(config-subif)#ip address 192.168.10.1 255.255.255.0`	Assigns the IP address and netmask.
`CORP(config-subif)#interface fastethernet 0/0.20`	Creates a virtual subinterface and moves to subinterface configuration mode.
`CORP(config-subif)#description Engineering VLAN 20`	Sets the locally significant interface description.
`CORP(config-subif)#encapsulation dot1q 20`	Assigns VLAN 20 to this subinterface. This subinterface uses the 802.1Q trunking protocol.
`CORP(config-subif)#ip address 192.168.20.1 255.255.255.0`	Assigns the IP address and netmask.
`CORP(config-subif)#interface fastethernet 0/0.30`	Creates a virtual subinterface and moves to subinterface configuration mode.

CORP(config-subif)#**description Marketing VLAN 30**	Sets the locally significant interface description.
CORP(config-subif)#**encapsulation dot1q 30**	Assigns VLAN 30 to this subinterface. This subinterface uses the 802.1Q trunking protocol.
CORP(config-subif)#**ip add 192.168.30.1 255.255.255.0**	Assigns the IP address and netmask.
CORP(config-subif)#**exit**	Returns to interface configuration mode.
CORP(config-if)#**exit**	Returns to global configuration mode.
CORP(config)#**router eigrp 10**	Creates EIGRP routing process 10 and moves to router configuration mode.
CORP(config-router)#**network 192.168.1.0**	Advertises the 192.168.1.0 network.
CORP(config-router)#**network 192.168.10.0**	Advertises the 192.168.10.0 network.
CORP(config-router)#**network 192.168.20.0**	Advertises the 192.168.20.0 network.
CORP(config-router)#**network 192.168.30.0**	Advertises the 192.168.30.0 network.
CORP(config-router)#**network 172.31.0.0**	Advertises the 172.31.0.0 network.
CORP(config-router)#**network 192.31.7.0**	Advertises the 192.31.7.0 network.
CORP(config-router)#**no auto-summary**	Turns off automatic summarization at classful boundary.
CORP(config-router)#**exit**	Returns to global configuration mode.
CORP(config)#**exit**	Returns to privileged mode.
CORP#**copy running-config startup-config**	Saves the configuration in NVRAM.

L2Switch2 (Catalyst 2960)

`Switch>`**`enable`**	Moves to privileged mode.
`Switch#`**`configure terminal`**	Moves to global configuration mode.
`Switch(config)#`**`hostname L2Switch2`**	Sets the host name.
`L2Switch2(config)#`**`vlan 10`**	Creates VLAN 10 and enters VLAN-configuration mode.
`L2Switch2(config-vlan)#`**`name Sales`**	Assigns a name to the VLAN.
`L2Switch2(config-vlan)#`**`exit`**	Returns to global configuration mode.
`L2Switch2(config)#`**`vlan 20`**	Creates VLAN 20 and enters VLAN-configuration mode.
`L2Switch2(config-vlan)#`**`name Engineering`**	Assigns a name to the VLAN.
`L2Switch2(config-vlan)#`**`vlan 30`**	Creates VLAN 30 and enters VLAN-configuration mode. Note that you do not have to exit back to global configuration mode to execute this command.
`L2Switch2(config-vlan)#`**`name Marketing`**	Assigns a name to the VLAN.
`L2Switch2(config-vlan)#`**`exit`**	Returns to global configuration mode.
`L2Switch2(config)#`**`interface range fastethernet 0/2 - 4`**	Enables you to set the same configuration parameters on multiple ports at the same time.
`L2Switch2(config-if-range)#`**`switchport mode access`**	Sets ports 2–4 as access ports.
`L2Switch2(config-if-range)#`**`switchport access vlan 10`**	Assigns ports 2–4 to VLAN 10.
`L2Switch2(config-if-range)#`**`interface range fastethernet 0/5 - 8`**	Enables you to set the same configuration parameters on multiple ports at the same time.
`L2Switch2(config-if-range)#`**`switchport mode access`**	Sets ports 5–8 as access ports.

`L2Switch2(config-if-range)#`**`switchport access vlan 20`**	Assigns ports 5–8 to VLAN 20.
`L2Switch2(config-if-range)#`**`interface range fastethernet 0/9 - 12`**	Enables you to set the same configuration parameters on multiple ports at the same time.
`L2Switch2(config-if-range)#`**`switchport mode access`**	Sets ports 9–12 as access ports.
`L2Switch2(config-if-range)#`**`switchport access vlan 30`**	Assigns ports 9–12 to VLAN 30.
`L2Switch2(config-if-range)#`**`exit`**	Returns to global configuration mode.
`L2Switch2(config)#`**`interface fastethernet 0/1`**	Moves to interface configuration mode.
`L2Switch2(config)#`**`description Trunk Link to CORP Router`**	Sets locally significant interface description.
`L2Switch2(config-if)#`**`switchport mode trunk`**	Puts the interface into trunking mode and negotiates to convert the link into a trunk link.
`L2Switch2(config-if)#`**`exit`**	Returns to global configuration mode.
`L2Switch2(config)#`**`interface vlan 1`**	Creates virtual interface for VLAN 1 and enters interface configuration mode.
`L2Switch2(config-if)#`**`ip address 192.168.1.2 255.255.255.0`**	Assigns the IP address and netmask.
`L2Switch2(config-if)#`**`no shutdown`**	Enables the interface.
`L2Switch2(config-if)#`**`exit`**	Returns to global configuration mode.
`L2Switch2(config)#`**`ip default-gateway 192.168.1.1`**	Assigns the default gateway address.
`L2Switch2(config)#`**`exit`**	Returns to privileged mode.
`L2Switch2#`**`copy running-config startup-config`**	Saves the configuration in NVRAM.

L3Switch1 (Catalyst 3560)

`Switch>`**`enable`**	Moves to privileged mode.
`Switch#`**`configure terminal`**	Moves to global configuration mode.
`Switch(config)#`**`hostname L3Switch1`**	Sets the host name.
`L3Switch1(config)#`**`vtp mode sever`**	Changes the switch to VTP server mode.
`L3Switch1(config)#`**`vtp domain testdomain`**	Configures the VTP domain name to testdomain.
`L3Switch1(config)#`**`vlan 10`**	Creates VLAN 10 and enters VLAN-configuration mode.
`L3Switch1(config-vlan)#`**`name Accounting`**	Assigns a name to the VLAN.
`L3Switch1(config-vlan)#`**`exit`**	Returns to global configuration mode.
`L3Switch1(config)#`**`vlan 20`**	Creates VLAN 20 and enters VLAN-configuration mode.
`L3Switch1(config-vlan)#`**`name Marketing`**	Assigns a name to the VLAN.
`L3Switch1(config-vlan)#`**`exit`**	Returns to global configuration mode.
`L3Switch1(config)#`**`interface gigabitethernet 0/1`**	Moves to interface configuration mode.
`L3Switch1(config-if)#`**`switchport trunk encapsulation dot1q`**	Specifies 802.1Q encapsulation on the trunk link.
`L3Switch1(config-if)#`**`switchport mode trunk`**	Puts the interface into trunking mode and negotiates to convert the link into a trunk link.
`L3Switch1(config-if)#`**`exit`**	Returns to global configuration mode.
`L3Switch1(config)#`**`ip routing`**	Enables IP routing on this device.
`L3Switch1(config)#`**`interface vlan 1`**	Creates a virtual interface for VLAN 1 and enters interface configuration mode.

L3Switch1(config-if)#**ip address 172.16.1.1 255.255.255.0**	Assigns the IP address and netmask.
L3Switch1(config-if)#**no shutdown**	Enables the interface.
L3Switch1(config-if)#**interface vlan 10**	Creates a virtual interface for VLAN 10 and enters interface configuration mode.
L3Switch1(config-if)#**ip address 172.16.10.1 255.255.255.0**	Assigns the IP address and mask.
L3Switch1(config-if)#**no shutdown**	Enables the interface.
L3Switch1(config-if)#**interface vlan 20**	Creates a virtual interface for VLAN 20 and enters interface configuration mode.
L3Switch1(config-if)#**ip address 172.16.20.1 255.255.255.0**	Assigns the IP address and mask.
L3Switch1(config-if)#**no shutdown**	Enables the interface.
L3Switch1(config-if)#**exit**	Returns to global configuration mode.
L3Switch1(config)#**interface fastethernet 0/24**	Enters interface configuration mode.
L3Switch1(config-if)#**no switchport**	Creates a Layer 3 port on the switch.
L3Switch1(config-if)#**ip address 172.31.1.6 255.255.255.252**	Assigns the IP address and netmask.
L3Switch1(config-if)#**exit**	Returns to global configuration mode.
L3Switch1(config)#**router eigrp 10**	Creates EIGRP routing process 10 and moves to router config mode.
L3Switch1(config-router)#**network 172.16.0.0**	Advertises the 172.16.0.0 classful network.
L3Switch1(config-router)#**network 172.31.0.0**	Advertises the 172.31.0.0 classful network.

`L3Switch1(config-router)#no auto-summary`	Turns off automatic summarization at classful boundary.
`L3Switch1(config-router)#exit`	Applies changes and returns to global configuration mode.
`L3Switch1(config)#exit`	Returns to privileged mode.
`L3Switch1#copy running-config startup-config`	Saves configuration in NVRAM.

L2Switch1 (Catalyst 2960)

`Switch>enable`	Moves to privileged mode.
`Switch#configure terminal`	Moves to global configuration mode.
`Switch(config)#hostname L2Switch1`	Sets the host name.
`L2Switch1(config)#vtp domain testdomain`	Configures the VTP domain name to testdomain.
`L2Switch1(config)#vtp mode client`	Changes the switch to VTP client mode.
`L2Switch1(config)#interface range fastethernet 0/1 - 4`	Enables you to set the same configuration parameters on multiple ports at the same time.
`L2Switch1(config-if-range)#switchport mode access`	Sets ports 1–4 as access ports.
`L2Switch1(config-if-range)#switchport access vlan 10`	Assigns ports 1–4 to VLAN 10.
`L2Switch1(config-if-range)#interface range fastethernet 0/5 - 8`	Enables you to set the same configuration parameters on multiple ports at the same time.
`L2Switch1(config-if-range)#switchport mode access`	Sets ports 5–8 as access ports.
`L2Switch1(config-if-range)#switchport access vlan 20`	Assigns ports 5–8 to VLAN 20.
`L2Switch1(config-if-range)#exit`	Returns to global configuration mode.

L2Switch1(config)#**interface gigabitethernet 0/1**	Moves to interface configuration mode.
L2Switch1(config-if)#**switchport mode trunk**	Puts the interface into trunking mode and negotiates to convert the link into a trunk link.
L2Switch1(config-if)#**exit**	Returns to global configuration mode.
L2Switch1(config)#**interface vlan 1**	Creates a virtual interface for VLAN 1 and enters interface configuration mode.
L2Switch1(config-if)#**ip address 172.16.1.2 255.255.255.0**	Assigns the IP address and netmask.
L2Switch1(config-if)#**no shutdown**	Enables the interface.
L2Switch1(config-if)#**exit**	Returns to global configuration mode.
L2Switch1(config)#**ip default-gateway 172.16.1.1**	Assigns the default gateway address.
L2Switch1(config)#**exit**	Returns to privileged mode.
L2Switch1#**copy running-config startup-config**	Saves the configuration in NVRAM.

Configuring DHCP Server on a Router or Layer 3 Switch

Router(config)#**ip dhcp pool internal**	Creates a DHCP pool called internal.
Router(dhcp-config)#**network 172.16.10.0 255.255.255.0**	Defines the range of addresses to be leased.
Router(dhcp-config)#**default-router 172.16.10.1**	Defines the address of the default router for the client.
Router(dhcp-config)#**dns-server 172.16.10.10**	Defines the address of the Domain Name System (DNS) server for the client.

`Router(dhcp-config)#`**`netbios-name-`** **`server 172.16.10.10`**	Defines the address of the NetBIOS server for the client.
`Router(dhcp-config)#`**`domain-name`** **`fakedomainname.ca`**	Defines the domain name for the client.
`Router(dhcp-config)#` **`lease 14 12 23`**	Defines the lease time to be 14 days, 12 hours, 23 minutes.
`Router(dhcp-config)#`**`lease infinite`**	Sets the lease time to infinity; the default time is 1 day.
`Router(dhcp-config)#`**`exit`**	Returns to global configuration mode.
`Router(config)#`**`ip dhcp excluded-address`** **`172.16.10.1 172.16.10.9`**	Specifies the range of addresses not to be leased out to clients.
`Router(config)#`**`service dhcp`**	Enables the DHCP service and relay features on a Cisco IOS router.
`Router(config)#`**`no service dhcp`**	Turns off the DHCP service. DHCP service is enabled by default in Cisco IOS Software.

Verifying and Troubleshooting DHCP Configuration

`Router#`**`show ip dhcp binding`**	Displays a list of all bindings created.
`Router#`**`show ip dhcp binding`** *`w.x.y.z`*	Displays the bindings for a specific DHCP client with an IP address of *w.x.y.z*.
`Router#`**`clear ip dhcp binding`** *`a.b.c.d`*	Clears an automatic address binding from the DHCP server database.
`Router#`**`clear ip dhcp binding *`**	Clears all automatic DHCP bindings.
`Router#`**`show ip dhcp conflict`**	Displays a list of all address conflicts recorded by the DHCP server.
`Router#`**`clear ip dhcp conflict`** *`a.b.c.d`*	Clears address conflict from the database.
`Router#`**`clear ip dhcp conflict *`**	Clears conflicts for all addresses.

Router#`show ip dhcp database`	Displays recent activity on the DHCP database.
Router#`show ip dhcp server statistics`	Displays a list of the number of messages sent and received by the DHCP server.
Router#`clear ip dhcp server statistics`	Resets all DHCP server counters to 0.
Router#`debug ip dhcp server {events ǀ packets ǀ linkage ǀ class}`	Displays the DHCP process of addresses being leased and returned.

Configuring a DHCP Helper Address

> **NOTE:** For the SVI line state to be up, at least one port in the VLAN must be up and forwarding. The **switchport auto-state exclude** command excludes a port from the SVI interface line-state up-or-down calculation.

Router

Router(config)#`interface fastethernet 0/0`	Moves to interface configuration mode.
Router(config-if)#`ip helper-address 172.16.20.2`	DHCP broadcasts will be forwarded as a unicast to this specific address rather than be dropped by the router.

Layer 3 Switch

Switch(config)#`interface vlan 10`	Moves to SVI configuration mode.
Switch(config-if)#`ip helper-address 172.16.20.2`	DHCP broadcasts will be forwarded as a unicast to this specific address rather than be dropped by the router.

> **NOTE:** The **ip helper-address** command forwards broadcast packets as a unicast to eight different UDP ports by default:
> - TFTP (port 69)
> - DNS (port 53)
> - Time service (port 37)

- NetBIOS name server (port 137)
- NetBIOS datagram server (port 138)
- Boot Protocol (BOOTP) client and server datagrams (ports 67 and 68)
- TACACS service (port 49)
- Host Name Service (port 42)

To close some of these ports, use the **no ip forward-protocol udp** *x* command at the global configuration prompt, where *x* is the port number you want to close. The following command stops the forwarding of broadcasts to port 49:

```
Router(config)#no ip forward-protocol udp 49
```

To open other UDP ports, use the **ip forward-helper udp** *x* command, where *x* is the port number you want to open:

```
Router(config)#ip forward-protocol udp 517
```

DHCP Client on a Cisco IOS Software Ethernet Interface

`Router(config)#interface fastethernet 0/0`	Moves to interface configuration mode.
`Router(config-if)#ip address dhcp`	Specifies that the interface acquire an IP address through DHCP.
	NOTE: The **ip address dhcp** command can also be applied on an L3 switch at the SVI as well as any port where the **no switchport** command has been used.

Configuration Example: DHCP

Figure 4-2 illustrates the network topology for the configuration that follows, which shows how to configure DHCP services on a Cisco IOS router using the commands covered in this chapter.

Figure 4-2   Network Topology for DHCP Configuration

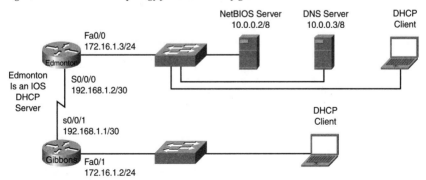

Edmonton Router

`router>`**`enable`**	Moves to privileged mode.
`router#`**`configure terminal`**	Moves to global configuration mode.
`router(config)#`**`host Edmonton`**	Sets the host name.
`Edmonton(config)#`**`interface fastethernet 0/0`**	Moves to interface configuration mode.
`Edmonton(config-if)#`**`description LAN Interface`**	Sets the local description of the interface.
`Edmonton(config-if)#`**`ip address 10.0.0.1 255.0.0.0`**	Assigns an IP address and netmask.
`Edmonton(config-if)#`**`no shutdown`**	Enables the interface.
`Edmonton(config-if)#`**`interface serial 0/0/0`**	Moves to interface configuration mode.
`Edmonton(config-if)#`**`description Link to Gibbons Router`**	Sets the local description of the interface.
`Edmonton(config-if)#`**`ip address 192.168.1.2 255.255.255.252`**	Assigns an IP address and netmask.
`Edmonton(config-if)#`**`clock rate 56000`**	Assigns the clock rate to the DCE cable on this side of link.
`Edmonton(config-if)#`**`no shutdown`**	Enables the interface.
`Edmonton(config-if)#`**`exit`**	Returns to global configuration mode.
`Edmonton(config)#`**`router eigrp 10`**	Enables the EIGRP routing process for autonomous system 10.
`Edmonton(config-router)#`**`network 10.0.0.0`**	Advertises the 10.0.0.0 network.
`Edmonton(config-router)#`**`network 192.168.1.0`**	Advertises the 192.168.1.0 network.
`Edmonton(config-router)#`**`exit`**	Returns to global configuration mode.
`Edmonton(config)#`**`service dhcp`**	Verifies that the router can use DHCP services and that DHCP is enabled.
`Edmonton(config)#`**`ip dhcp excluded-address 10.0.0.1 10.0.0.5`**	Specifies the range of addresses not to be leased out to clients.

`Edmonton(config)#ip dhcp pool 10 network`	Creates a DHCP pool called 10network.
`Edmonton(dhcp-config)#network 10.0.0.0 255.0.0.0`	Defines the range of addresses to be leased.
`Edmonton(dhcp-config)#default-router 10.0.0.1`	Defines the address of the default router for clients.
`Edmonton(dhcp-config)#netbios-name-server 10.0.0.2`	Defines the address of the NetBIOS server for clients.
`Edmonton(dhcp-config)#dns-server 10.0.0.3`	Defines the address of the DNS server for clients.
`Edmonton(dhcp-config)#domain-name fakedomainname.ca`	Defines the domain name for clients.
`Edmonton(dhcp-config)#lease 12 14 30`	Sets the lease time to be 12 days, 14 hours, 30 minutes.
`Edmonton(dhcp-config)#exit`	Returns to global configuration mode.
`Edmonton(config)#ip dhcp pool 192.168.3network`	Creates a DHCP pool called the 192.168.3network.
`Edmonton(dhcp-config)#network 192.168.3.0 255.255.255.0`	Defines the range of addresses to be leased.
`Edmonton(dhcp-config)#default-router 192.168.3.1`	Defines the address of the default router for clients.
`Edmonton(dhcp-config)#netbios-name-server 10.0.0.2`	Defines the address of the NetBIOS server for clients.
`Edmonton(dhcp-config)#dns-server 10.0.0.3`	Defines the address of the DNS server for clients.
`Edmonton(dhcp-config)#domain-name fakedomainname.ca`	Defines the domain name for clients.
`Edmonton(dhcp-config)#lease 12 14 30`	Sets the lease time to be 12 days, 14 hours, 30 minutes.
`Edmonton(dhcp-config)#exit`	Returns to global configuration mode.
`Edmonton(config)#exit`	Returns to privileged mode.
`Edmonton#copy running-config startup-config`	Saves the configuration to NVRAM.

Gibbons Router

router>**enable**	Enters privileged mode.
router#**configure terminal**	Enters global configuration mode.
router(config)#**host Gibbons**	Sets the host name.
Gibbons(config)#**interface fastethernet 0/0**	Enters interface configuration mode.
Gibbons(config-if)#**description LAN Interface**	Sets the local description of the interface.
Gibbons(config-if)#**ip address 192.168.3.1 255.255.255.0**	Assigns an IP address and netmask.
Gibbons(config-if)#**ip helper-address 192.168.1.2**	DHCP broadcasts will be forwarded as a unicast to this address rather than be dropped.
Gibbons(config-if)#**no shutdown**	Enables the interface.
Gibbons(config-if)#**interface serial 0/0/1**	Enters interface configuration mode.
Gibbons(config-if)#**description Link to Edmonton Router**	Sets the local description of the interface.
Gibbons(config-if)#**ip address 192.168.1.1 255.255.255.252**	Assigns an IP address and netmask.
Gibbons(config-if)#**no shutdown**	Enables the interface.
Gibbons(config-if)#**exit**	Returns to global configuration mode.
Gibbons(config)#**router eigrp 10**	Enables the EIGRP routing process for autonomous system 10.
Gibbons(config-router)#**network 192.168.3.0**	Advertises the 192.168.3.0 network.
Gibbons(config-router)#**network 192.168.1.0**	Advertises the 192.168.1.0 network.
Gibbons(config-router)#**exit**	Returns to global configuration mode.
Gibbons(config)#**exit**	Returns to privileged mode.
Gibbons#**copy running-config startup-config**	Saves the configuration to NVRAM.

NOTE: The subnets of the VLANs are directly connected to the switch. Routing between these subnets does not require a dynamic routing protocol. If the switch is to be connected to a router and remote communication is desired, a routing protocol must be enabled and networks advertised:

```
3750Switch(config)#router eigrp 1
3750Switch(config-router)#network 172.16.0.0
3750Switch(config-router)#exit
3750Switch(config)#
```

Configuring Cisco Express Forwarding

Switch(config)#ip cef	Enables standard CEF.
Switch(config)#ip cef distributed	Enables distributed CEF (dCEF).
Switch(config)#no ip cef	Disables CEF globally.
Switch(config)#interface fastethernet 0/1	Moves to interface configuration mode.
Switch(config-if)#ip route-cache cef	Enables CEF on the interface.

Verifying CEF

Switch#show ip cef	Displays entries in the Forwarding Information Base (FIB).
Switch#show ip cef summary	Displays a summary of the FIB.
Switch#show ip cef unresolved	Displays unresolved FIB entries.
Switch#show ip cef fastethernet 0/1	Displays the FIB entry for the specified interface.
Switch#show ip cef fastethernet 0/1 detail	Displays detailed information about the FIB for the interface.
Switch#show interface fastethernet 0/1 | begin L3	Displays switching statistics for the interface beginning at the section for L3.

Switch#**show interface gigabitethernet 1/1** | include **switched**	Displays switching statistics that show statistics for each layer.
Switch#**show adjacency fastethernet 0/20 detail**	Displays the content of the information to be used during L2 encapsulation.
	NOTE: When using the **show adjacency interface xx detail** command, both the next hop-hop and local MAC addresses are displayed as well as the well-known Ethertype value of the encapsulation protocol (0x0800 for IP).
Switch#**show cef drop**	Displays packets that are dropped because adjacencies are incomplete or nonexistent.
Switch#**show ip interface vlan10**	Verifies whether CEF is enabled on an interface.

Troubleshooting CEF

Switch#**debug ip cef**	Displays debug information for CEF.
Switch#**debug ip cef drops**	Displays debug information about dropped packets.
Switch#**debug ip cef drops** *x*	Records CEF dropped packets that match access-list x.
Switch#**debug ip cef receive**	Displays packets that are not switched using information from the FIB but that are received and sent to the next switching layer.
Switch#**debug ip cef events**	Displays general CEF events.
Switch#**debug ip cef prefix-ipc**	Displays updates related to IP prefix information.
Switch#**debug ip cef table**	Produces a table showing events related to the FIB table.
Switch#**ping ip**	Performs an extended ping.

CHAPTER 5

Implementing a Highly Available Network

This chapter provides information and commands concerning the following topics:

- Implementing network logging
- Service Level Agreements (SLA)

Implementing Network Logging

Configuring Syslog

Cisco routers and switches are capable of logging information relating to a number of different kinds of events that occur—configuration changes, ACL violations, interface status, and so on. Cisco network devices can direct these log messages to several different locations: console, terminal lines, memory buffers, SNMP traps, or an external syslog server.

To get the most out of your device log messages, it is imperative that your devices display the correct time; using NTP helps facilitate your routers all having the correct time.

Messages are listed by the facility (hardware device, protocol, or a module or system software) that produces the messages. Within each facility, messages are listed by the severity level, from highest to lowest and a description mnemonic. Each message is followed by an explanation and a recommended action.

Figure 5-1 shows the message structure and format of Cisco network device System Message Log messages.

Figure 5-1   System Message Log Message Structure

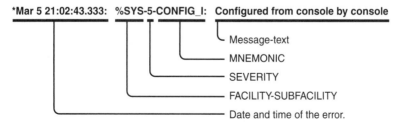

*Mar 5 21:02:43.333:   %SYS-5-CONFIG_I: Configured from console by console

- Message-text
- MNEMONIC
- SEVERITY
- FACILITY-SUBFACILITY
- Date and time of the error.

There are eight levels of severity in logging messages:

Level	Name	Definition	Example
0	emergencies	System is unusable	Cisco IOS Software could not load
1	alerts	Immediate action needed	Temperature too high
2	critical	Critical conditions	Unable to allocate memory
3	errors	Error conditions	Invalid memory size
4	warnings	Warning conditions	Crypto operation failed
5	notifications	Normal but significant conditions	Interface changed state, up or down
6	informational	Informational messages	Packet denied by ACL (default)
7	debugging	Debugging messages	Packet type invalid

Setting a level means you will get that level and everything below it. For example, Level 6 means you will receive Level 6 down to Level 0 messages. Level 4 means you will get messages for Levels 4–0. The default reporting level is typically Level 7 (debugging).

`Switch(config)#`**`logging on`**	Enables logging to all supported destinations.
`Switch(config)#`**`logging buffered warnings`**	Enables local logging for events that are warnings and more serious.
`Switch(config)#`**`logging buffered 4096`**	Creates a local logging buffer of 4096 bytes.
`Switch(config)#`**`logging 192.168.10.53`**	Sends logging messages to a syslog server host at address 192.168.10.53.
	NOTE: This is equivalent to the **logging host** command.
`Switch(config)#`**`logging sysadmin`**	Sends logging messages to a syslog server host named sysadmin.

Switch(config)#**logging trap** *x*	Sets the syslog server logging level to value *x*, where *x* = a number between 0 and 7 or a word defining the level.
Switch(config)#**logging source-interface loopback 0**	Sets the source IP address of the syslog packets, regardless of the interface where the packets actually exit the router.
Switch(config)#**service timestamps log datetime**	Includes a timestamp in all subsequent syslog messages.

CAUTION: If any debugging is enabled and the logging buffer is configured to include Level 7 (debugging) messages, the debug output will be included in the system log.

Switch#**show logging**	Displays the local logs and some current settings.

Configuring an SNMP Managed Node

Switch#**configure terminal**	Enters global configuration mode.
Switch(config)#**access-list 10 permit ip 10.1.1.0 0.0.0.255**	Configures an access list to define the managing IP segment(s).
Switch(config)#**snmp-server community CISCONET2**	Configures the community string.
Switch(config)#**snmp-server community CISCONET2 ro 10**	Optionally specifies either read-only (ro) or read-write (rw) if you want authorized management stations to retrieve and modify MIB objects. Optionally specifies an access list permitting management traffic.

	NOTE: By default, the community string permits read-only access to all objects.
`Switch(config)#`**`snmp-server engineID local 1234567890`**	Sets a string to identify the local device as 1234567890.
	NOTE: Engine ID must be 10 hexadecimal characters or more.
`Switch(config)#`**`snmp-server group scottgroup v3 auth`**	Defines an SNMP group named scottgroup for SNMPv3 using authentication.
`Switch(config)#`**`snmp-server group hansgroup v3 priv`**	Defines an SNMP group named hansgroup for SNMPv3 using authentication and encryption (privacy).
`Switch(config)#`**`snmp-server user Scott scottgroup v3 auth md5 scott2passwd`**	Defines a user Scott belonging to the group scottgroup. Authentication uses MD5 for the password scott2passwd. No encryption parameters are set.
`Switch(config)#`**`snmp-server user Hans hansgroup v3 auth md5 hans2passwd priv des    password2`**	Defines a user Hans belonging to the group hansgroup. Authentication uses MD5 for the password hans2passwd. Encryption parameters use 56-bit DES with a password of password2.
	NOTE: The **snmp-server user** command is specific to the 6500 platform.

Switch(config)#**snmp-server host 172.16.31.200 inform version 3 noauth Hans**	Specifies the recipient—172.16.31.200—of an SNMP notification in the form of an inform. The SNMPv3 security level of noauth is used. The username is Hans.

Service Level Agreements (SLA)

Configuring IP SLA (Catalyst 3750)

Cisco IOS IP SLAs sends data across the network to measure performance between multiple network locations or network paths. It simulates network data and IP services and collects network performance information in real time. IP SLAs can send also SNMP traps that are triggered by events such as the following:

- Connection loss
- Timeout
- Round-trip time threshold
- Average jitter threshold
- One-way packet loss
- One-way jitter
- One-way mean opinion score (MOS)
- One-way latency

Figure 5-2 is the network topology for the IP SLA commands.

Figure 5-2   SLA Network Topology

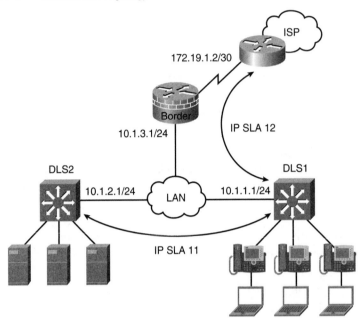

DLS1#**configure terminal**	Enters global configuration mode.
DLS1(config)#**ip sla 11**	Creates an IP SLAs operation and enter IP SLAs configuration mode.
DLS1(config-ip-sla)#**icmp-echo 10.1.2.1 source-ip 10.1.1.1**	Configures the IP SLAs operation as an ICMP Echo operation and enter ICMP echo configuration mode.
	NOTE: The ICMP ECHO operation does not require the IP SLAs responder to be enabled.
DLS1(config-ip-sla-echo)#**frequency 5**	Sets the rate at which the IP SLAs operation repeats.
DLS1(config-ip-sla-echo)#**exit**	Exits sla-echo configuration mode.

`DLS1(config)#`**`ip sla schedule 11 start-time now life forever`**	Configures the IP SLAs operation scheduling parameters to start now and continue forever.
	NOTE: The start time for the SLA can be set to a particular time and day, to be recurring, to be activated after a threshold is passed, and kept as an active process for a configurable number of seconds.
`DLS2(config)#`**`ip sla responder udp-echo ipaddress 10.1.1.1 port 10000`**	Configures switch DLS2 as an IP SLA responder with 10.1.1.1 using UDP port 10000.
`DLS1(config)#`**`ip sla 12`**	Creates an IP SLAs operation and enters IP SLAs configuration mode.
`DLS1(config-ip-sla)#`**`path-jitter 172.19.1.2 source-ip 10.1.1.1`**	Configures the IP SLAs operation as a path-jitter operation and enters path-jitter configuration mode.
	NOTE: The path-jitter SLA sends 10 packets per operation with a 20 ms time interval between them by default.
`DLS1(config-ip-sla-pathJitter)#`**`frequency 5`**	Sets the rate at which the IP SLAs operation repeats.
`DLS1(config-ip-sla-pathJitter)#`**`tos 0x80`**	Sets the type of service to value to 0x80.
`DLS1(config-ip-sla-pathJitter)#`**`exit`**	Exits path-jitter configuration mode.
`DLS1(config)# DLS1(config)#`**`ip sla schedule 12 recurring start-time 07:00 life 3600`**	Configures the IP SLAs operation scheduling parameters to start at 7:00 AM and continue for 1 hour every day.

Monitoring IP SLA Operations

Switch#**show ip sla application**	Displays global information about Cisco IOS IP SLAs.
	NOTE: The **show ip sla application** command displays supported SLA operation types and supported SLA protocols.
Switch#**show ip sla configuration x**	Displays configuration values including all defaults for operation "x"
Switch#**show ip sla statistics**	Displays current or aggregated operational status and statistics.

Chapter 6

Implementing a First Hop Redundancy Protocols Solution

This chapter provides information and commands concerning the following topics:

- Hot Standby Routing Protocol (HSRP)
  - Configuring HSRP
  - Default HSRP configuration settings
  - Verifying HSRP
  - HSRP optimization options
  - Multiple HSRP groups
  - HSRP IP SLA tracking
  - Debugging HSRP
- Virtual Router Redundancy Protocol (VRRP)
  - Configuring VRRP
  - Verifying VRRP
  - Debugging VRRP
- Gateway Load Balancing Protocol (GLBP)
  - Configuring GLBP
  - Verifying GLBP
  - Debugging GLBP
- Configuration example: HSRP on L3 Switch
- Configuration example: GLBP

Hot Standby Routing Protocol

The Hot Standby Routing Protocol (HSRP) provides network redundancy for IP networks, ensuring that user traffic immediately and transparently recovers from first-hop failures in network edge devices or access circuits.

When configuring HSRP on a switch platform, the specified interface must be a Layer 3 interface:

- **Routed port**—A physical port configured as a Layer 3 port by entering the **no switchport** interface configuration command
- **SVI**—A VLAN interface created by using the **interface vlan vlan_id** global configuration command and, by default, a Layer 3 interface
- **EtherChannel port channel in Layer 3 mode**—A port-channel logical interface created by using the **interface port-channel port-channel-number** global configuration command and binding the Ethernet interface into the channel group

Configuring HSRP

`Switch(config)#interface fastethernet 0/0`	Moves to interface configuration mode.
`Switch(config)#interface vlan 10`	Moves to interface configuration mode.
`Switch(config-if)#ip address 172.16.0.10 255.255.255.0`	Assigns IP address and netmask.
`Switch(config-if)#standby 1 ip 172.16.0.1`	Activates HSRP group 1 on the interface and creates a virtual IP address of 172.16.0.1 for use in HSRP.
	NOTE: The group number can be from 0 to 255. The default is 0.
`Switch(config-if)#standby 1 priority 120`	Assigns a priority value of 120 to standby group 1.
	NOTE: The priority value can be from 1 to 255. The default is 100. A higher priority results in that switch being elected the active switch. If the priorities of all switches in the group are equal, the switch with the *highest IP address* becomes the active switch.

Default HSRP Configuration Settings

Feature	Default Setting
HSRP version	Version 1
	NOTE: HSRPv1 and HSRPv2 have different packet structure. The same HSRP version must be configured on all devices of an HSRP group.
HSRP groups	None configured
Standby group number	0
Standby MAC address	System assigned as 0000.0c07.ac*XX*, where *XX* is the HSRP group number
Standby priority	100
Standby delay	0 (no delay)
Standby track interface priority	10
Standby hello time	3 seconds
Standby holdtime	10 seconds

Verifying HSRP

`Switch#`**`show running-config`**	Displays what is currently running on the switch.
`Switch#`**`show standby`**	Displays HSRP information.
`Switch#`**`show standby brief`**	Displays a single-line output summary of each standby group.
`Switch#`**`show standby vlan 1`**	Displays HSRP information on the VLAN 1 group.

HSRP Optimization Options

There are options available that make it possible to optimize HSRP operation in the campus network. The next three sections explain three of these options: standby preempt, message timers, and interface tracking.

Preempt

`Switch(config)#`**`interface vlan 10`**	Moves to interface configuration mode.
`Switch(config-if)#`**`standby 1 preempt`**	Preempts, or takes control of, the active switch if the local priority is higher than the active switch.
`Switch(config-if)#`**`standby 1 preempt delay minimum 180`**	Causes the local switch to postpone taking over as the active switch for 180 seconds since that switch was last restarted.
`Switch(config-if)#`**`standby 1 preempt delay reload`**	Enables preemption to occur only after a switch reloads.
`Switch(config-if)#`**`no standby 1 preempt delay reload`**	Disables the preemption delay, but preemption itself is still enabled. Use the **no standby** x **preempt** command to eliminate preemption.
	NOTE: If the **preempt** argument is not configured, the local switch assumes control as the active switch only if the local switch receives information indicating that there is no switch currently in the active state.

HSRP Message Timers

`Switch(config)#`**`interface vlan 10`**	Moves to interface config mode.
`Switch(config-if)#`**`standby 1 timers 5 15`**	Sets the hello timer to 5 seconds and sets the hold timer to 15 seconds.
	NOTE: The hold timer is normally set to be greater than or equal to three times the hello timer.
	NOTE: The hello timer can be from 1 to 254; the default is 3. The hold timer can be from 1 to 255; the default is 10. The default unit of time is seconds.
`Switch(config-if)#`**`standby 1 timers msec 200 msec 600`**	Sets the hello timer to 200 milliseconds and sets the hold timer to 600 milliseconds.
	NOTE: If the **msec** argument is used, the timers can be an integer from 15 to 999.

Interface Tracking

`Switch(config)#`**`interface vlan 10`**	Moves to interface configuration mode.
`Switch(config-if)#`**`standby 1 track fastethernet 0/0 25`**	HSRP tracks the availability of interface FastEthernet 0/0. If FastEthernet 0/0 goes down, the priority of the switch in group 1 is decremented by 25.
	NOTE: The default value of the **track** argument is 10.
	TIP: The **track** argument does not assign a new priority if the tracked interface goes down. The **track** argument assigns a value that the priority will be decreased if the tracked interface goes down. Therefore, if you are tracking FastEthernet 0/0 with a track value of 25— **standby 1 track serial 0/0 25**—and FastEthernet 0/0 goes down, the priority is decreased by 25; assuming a default priority of 100, the new priority will now be 75.

Multiple HSRP

Figure 6-1 shows the network topology for the configuration that follows, which shows two HSRP groups with a different active forwarder for each VLAN.

Figure 6-1   Network Topology for MHSRP Configuration Example

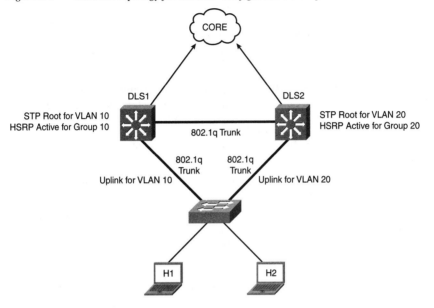

`DLS1(config)#spanning-tree` `vlan 10 root primary`	Configures spanning-tree root primary for VLAN 10.
`DLS1(config)#spanning-tree` `vlan 20 root secondary`	Configures spanning-tree root primary for VLAN 20.
	NOTE: Load balancing is accomplished by having one switch as the active HSRP L3-Switch forwarding for half of the VLANs and the standby L3-Switch for the remaining VLANs. The second HSRP L3-Switch is reversed in its active and standby VLANs. Care must be taken to ensure that spanning-tree is forwarding to the active L3-Switch for the correct VLANs by making that L3-Switch the Spanning-Tree Primary Root for those VLANs.
`DLS1(config)#interface vlan` `10`	Moves to interface configuration mode.

DLS1(config-if)#**ip address 10.1.10.2 255.255.255.0**	Assigns an IP address and netmask.
DLS1(config-if)#**standby 10 ip 10.1.10.1**	Activates HSRP group 10 on the interface and creates a virtual IP address of 10.1.10.1 for use in HSRP.
DLS1(config-if)#**standby 10 priority 110**	Assigns a priority value of 110 to standby group 10. This is the active forwarding switch for VLAN 10.
DLS1(config-if)#**standby 10 preempt**	Preempts, or takes control of, VLAN 10 forwarding if the local priority is higher than the active switch VLAN 1 priority.
DLS1(config-if)#**interface vlan 20**	Moves to interface configuration mode.
DLS1(config-if)#**ip address 10.1.20.2 255.255.255.0**	Assigns an IP address and netmask.
DLS1(config-if)#**standby 20 ip 10.1.20.1**	Activates HSRP group 20 on the interface and creates a virtual IP address of 10.1.20.1 for use in HSRP.
DLS1(config-if)#**standby 20 priority 90**	Assigns a priority value of 90 to standby group 20. This switch is the standby device for VLAN 20.
DLS1(config-if)#**standby 20 preempt**	Preempts, or takes control of, VLAN 20 forwarding if the local priority is higher than the active switch VLAN 20 priority.

HSRP IP SLA Tracking

switch(config)#**ip sla 10**	Creates SLA process 10.
switch(config-sla)#**icmp-echo 172.19.10.1**	Configures the SLA as an ICMP Echo operation to destination 172.19.10.1.
switch(config-sla)#**exit**	Exits SLA configuration mode.
switch(config)#**ip sla schedule 10 start-time now life forever**	Configures the scheduling for SLA 10 to start now and continue indefinitely.
	NOTE: The **ip sla schedule** command is the same as the **SLA schedule** command in Chapter 5, "Implementing a Highly Available Network."

`switch(config)#`**`track 90 ip`** **`sla 10 state`**	Creates an object, 90, to track the state of SLA process 10.
`switch(config)#`**`interface`** **`vlan 10`**	Moves to interface configuration mode.
`switch(config-if)#`**`ip address`** **`192.168.10.1 255.255.255.0`**	Assigns IP address and netmask.
`switch(config-if)#`**`standby 10`** **`ip 192.168.10.254`**	Activates HSRP group 10 on the interface and creates a virtual IP address of 192.168.10.254 for use in HSRP.
`switch(config-if)#`**`standby 10`** **`priority 110`**	Assigns a priority value of 110 to standby group 10.
`switch(config-if)#`**`standby 10`** **`preempt`**	Preempts, or takes control of, the active switch if the local priority is higher than the active switch.
`switch(config-if)#`**`standby 10`** **`track 90 decrement 20`**	Tracks the state of object 90 and decrements the device priority if the object fails.

Debugging HSRP

`Switch#`**`debug standby`**	Displays all HSRP debugging information, including state changes and transmission/reception of HSRP packets.
`Switch#`**`debug standby errors`**	Displays HSRP error messages.
`Switch#`**`debug standby events`**	Displays HSRP event messages.
`Switch#`**`debug standby events`** **`terse`**	Displays all HSRP events except for hellos and advertisements.
`Switch#`**`debug standby events`** **`track`**	Displays all HSRP tracking events.
`Switch#`**`debug standby packets`**	Displays HSRP packet messages.
`Switch#`**`debug standby terse`**	Displays all HSRP errors, events, and packets, except for hellos and advertisements.

Virtual Router Redundancy Protocol

> **NOTE:** HSRP is Cisco proprietary. The Virtual Router Redundancy Protocol (VRRP) is an IEEE standard.

> **NOTE:** The VRRP is not supported on the Catalyst 3750-E, 3750, 3560, or 3550 platforms. VRRP is supported on the Catalyst 4500 and Catalyst 6500 platforms.

VRRP is an election protocol that dynamically assigns responsibility for one or more virtual switches to the VRRP switches on a LAN, enabling several switches on a multiaccess link to use the same virtual IP address. A VRRP switch is configured to run VRRP in conjunction with one or more other switches attached.

Configuring VRRP

`Switch(config)#interface vlan 10`	Moves to interface configuration mode.
`Switch(config-if)#ip address 172.16.100.5 255.255.255.0`	Assigns IP address and netmask.
`Switch(config-if)#vrrp 10 ip 172.16.100.1`	Enables VRRP for group 10 on this interface with a virtual address of 172.16.100.1. The group number can be from 1 to 255.
`Switch(config-if)#vrrp 10 description Engineering Group`	Assigns a text description to the group.
`Switch(config-if)#vrrp 10 priority 110`	Sets the priority level for this VLAN. The range is from 1 to 254. The default is 100.
`Switch(config-if)#vrrp 10 preempt`	Preempts, or takes over, as the virtual switch master for group 10 if it has a higher priority than the current virtual switch master.
`Switch(config-if)#vrrp 10 preempt delay 60`	Preempts, but only after a delay of 60 seconds.
	NOTE: The default delay period is 0 seconds.
`Switch(config-if)#vrrp 10 timers advertise 15`	Configures the interval between successful advertisements by the virtual switch master.
	NOTE: The default interval value is 1 second.

	NOTE: All switches in a VRRP group must use the same timer values. If switches have different timer values set, the VRRP group does not communicate with each other.
	NOTE: The range of the advertisement timer is 1 to 255 seconds. If you use the **msec** argument, you change the timer to measure in milliseconds. The range in milliseconds is 50 to 999.
`Switch(config-if)#`**`vrrp 10 timers learn`**	Configures the switch, when acting as a virtual switch backup, to learn the advertisement interval used by the virtual switch master.
`Switch(config-if)#`**`vrrp 10 shutdown`**	Disables VRRP on the interface, but configuration is still retained.
`Switch(config-if)#`**`no vrrp 10 shutdown`**	Reenables the VRRP group using the previous configuration.

Verifying VRRP

`Switch#`**`show running-config`**	Displays the contents of dynamic RAM.
`Switch#`**`show vrrp`**	Displays VRRP information.
`Switch#`**`show vrrp brief`**	Displays a brief status of all VRRP groups.
`Switch#`**`show vrrp all`**	Displays detailed information about all VRRP groups, including groups in the disabled state.
`Switch#`**`show vrrp interface vlan 10`**	Displays information about VRRP as enabled on interface VLAN 10.
`Switch#`**`show vrrp interface vlan 10 brief`**	Displays a brief summary about VRRP on interface VLAN 10.

Debugging VRRP

`Switch#`**`debug vrrp all`**	Displays all VRRP messages.
`Switch#`**`debug vrrp error`**	Displays all VRRP error messages.
`Switch#`**`debug vrrp events`**	Displays all VRRP event messages.
`Switch#`**`debug vrrp packets`**	Displays messages about packets sent and received.
`Switch#`**`debug vrrp state`**	Displays messages about state transitions.

Gateway Load Balancing Protocol

Gateway Load Balancing Protocol (GLBP) protects data traffic from a failed router or circuit, like HSRP and VRRP, while allowing packet load sharing between a group of redundant routers.

Configuring GLBP

`Router(config)#interface` `fastethernet 0/0`	Moves to interface config mode.
`Router(config)#interface` `vlan 10`	Moves to interface config mode.
`Router(config-if)#ip address` `172.16.100.5 255.255.255.0`	Assigns an IP address and netmask.
`Router(config-if)#glbp 10 ip` `172.16.100.1`	Enables GLBP for group 10 on this interface with a virtual address of 172.16.100.1. The range of group numbers is from 0 to 1023.
`Router(config-if)#glbp 10` `preempt`	Configures the switch to preempt, or take over, as the active virtual gateway (AVG) for group 10 if this switch has a higher priority than the current AVG.
`Router(config-if)#glbp 10` `preempt delay minimum 60`	Configures the router to preempt, or take over, as AVG for group 10 if this router has a higher priority than the current active virtual forwarder (AVF) after a delay of 60 seconds.
`Router(config-if)#glbp 10` `forwarder preempt`	Configures the router to preempt, or take over, as AVF for group 10 if this router has a higher priority than the current AVF. This command is enabled by default with a delay of 30 seconds.
`Router(config-if)#glbp 10` `preempt delay minimum 60`	Configures the router to preempt, or take over, as AVF for group 10 if this router has a higher priority than the current AVF after a delay of 60 seconds.

	NOTE: Members of a GLBP group elect one gateway to be the AVG for that group. Other group members provide backup for the AVG in case the AVG becomes unavailable. The AVG assigns a virtual MAC address to each member of the GLBP group. Each gateway assumes responsibility for forwarding packets sent to the virtual MAC address assigned to it by the AVG. These gateways are known as AVFs for their virtual MAC address. Virtual forwarder redundancy is similar to virtual gateway redundancy with an AVF. If the AVF fails, one of the secondary virtual forwarders in the listen state assumes responsibility for the virtual MAC address.
	NOTE: The **glbp preempt** command uses priority to determine what happens if the AVG fails as well as the order of ascendancy to becoming an AVG if the current AVG fails. The **glbp forwarder preempt** command uses weighting value to determine the forwarding capacity of each router in the GLBP group.
Router(config-if)#**glbp 10 priority 150**	Sets the priority level of the switch.
	NOTE: The range of the **priority** argument is 1 to 255. The default priority of GLBP is 100. A higher priority number is preferred.
Router(config-if)#**glbp 10 timers 5 15**	Configures the hello timer to be set to 5 seconds and the hold timer to be 15 seconds.
Router(config-if)#**glbp 10 timers msec 20200 msec 60600**	Configures the hello timer to be 20200 milliseconds and the hold timer to be 60600 milliseconds.
	NOTE: The default hello timer is 3 seconds. The range of the hello timer interval is 1 to 60 seconds. If the **msec** argument is used, the timer is measured in milliseconds, with a range of 50 to 60000.

	NOTE: The default hold timer is 10 seconds. The range of the hold timer is 1 to 180 seconds. If the **msec** argument is used, the timer is measured in milliseconds, with a range of 70 to 180000.
	The hello timer measures the interval between successive hello packets sent by the AVG in a GLBP group. The **holdtime** argument specifies the interval before the virtual gateway and the virtual forwarder information in the hello packet is considered invalid. It is recommended that, unless you are extremely familiar with your network design and with the mechanisms of GLBP, you do not change the timers. To reset the timers to their default values, use the **no glbp** *x* **timers** command, where *x* is the GLBP group number.
`Router(config-if)#glbp 10 load-balancing host-dependent`	Specifies that GLBP will load balance using the host-dependent method.
`Router(config-if)#glbp 10 load-balancing weighted`	Specifies that GLBP loads balance using the weighted method.
`Router(config-if)#glbp 10 weighting 80`	Assigns a maximum weighting value for this interface for load balancing purposes. The value can be from 1 to 254.
`Router(config-if)#glbp 10 load-balancing round-robin`	Specifies that GLBP loads balance using the round-robin method.

NOTE: There are three different types of load balancing in GLBP:

- Host-dependent uses the MAC address of a host to determine which VF MAC address the host is directed toward. This is used with stateful Network Address Translation (NAT) because NAT requires each host to be returned to the same virtual MAC address each time it sends an ARP request for the virtual IP address. It is not recommended for situations where there are a small number of end hosts (fewer than 20).
- Weighted enables GLBP to place a weight on each device when calculating the amount of load sharing. For example, if there are two routers in the group, and router A has twice the forwarding capacity of router B, the weighting value should be configured to be double the amount of router B. To assign a weighting value, use the **glbp** *x* **weighting** *y* **interface** configuration command, where *x* is the GLBP group number and *y* is the weighting value, a number from 1 to 254.
- Round-robin load balancing occurs when each VF MAC address is used sequentially in ARP replies for the virtual IP address. Round-robin is suitable for any number of end hosts.

If no load balancing is used with GLBP, GLBP operates in an identical manner to HSRP, where the AVG only responds to ARP requests with its own VF MAC address, and all traffic is directed to the AVG.

Verifying GLBP

Router#**show running-config**	Displays the contents of dynamic RAM.
Router#**show glbp**	Displays GLBP information.
Router#**show glbp brief**	Displays a brief status of all GLBP groups.
Router#**show glbp 10**	Displays information about GLBP group 10.
Router#**show glbp vlan 10**	Displays GLBP information on interface VLAN 10.
Router#**show glbp vlan 20 10**	Displays GLBP group 10 information on interface VLAN 20.

Debugging GLBP

Router#**debug condition glbp**	Displays GLBP condition messages.
Router#**debug glbp errors**	Displays all GLBP error messages.
Router#**debug glbp events**	Displays all GLBP event messages.
Router#**debug glbp packets**	Displays messages about packets sent and received.
Router#**debug glbp terse**	Displays a limited range of debugging messages.

Configuration Example: HSRP on L3 Switch

Figure 6-2 shows the network topology for the configuration that follows, which shows how to configure HSRP using the commands covered in this chapter. Note that the example shows only the commands specific to HSRP.

Figure 6-2   Network Topology for HSRP Configuration Example

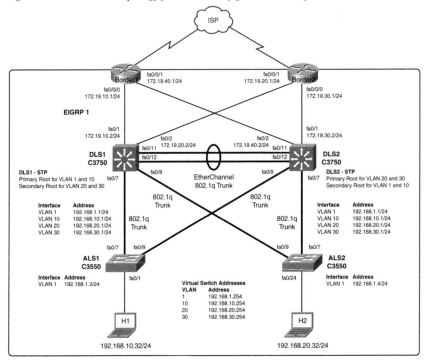

The network devices are configured as follows:

- DLS1 and DLS2 are configured as Layer 3 devices; ALS1 and ALS2 are configured as Layer 2 devices.

- Border1, Border2, DLS1, and DLS2 run EIGRP. Border1 and Border2 also provide default routing into the cloud.

- The links between DLS1, DLS2, Border1, and Border2 are routed links using the **no switchport** command on DLS1 and DLS2.

- Four VLANs are configured on DLS1. DLS1 is the VTP server for DLS2, ALS1, and ALS2.

- A Layer 2 EtherChannel connects DLS1 and DLS2.

- All connections between DLS1, DLS2, ALS1, and ALS2 are 802.1Q trunks.

- DLS1 is the spanning-tree primary root for VLAN 1 and 10, and DLS2 is the secondary root for VLAN 20 and 30.

- DLS2 is the spanning-tree primary root for VLAN 20 and 30, and DLS1 is the secondary root for VLAN 1 and 10.

Switch DLS1

DLS1(config)#`interface vlan 1`	Moves to interface configuration mode.
DLS1(config-if)#`standby 1 ip 192.168.1.254`	Activates HSRP group 1 on the interface and creates a virtual IP address of 192.168.1.254 for use in HSRP.
DLS1(config-if)#`standby 1 priority 105`	Assigns a priority value of 105 to standby group 1.
DLS1(config-if)#`standby 1 preempt`	Preempts, or takes control of, VLAN 1 forwarding if the local priority is higher than the active switch VLAN 1 priority.
DLS1(config-if)#`standby 1 track fastEthernet 0/1 20`	HSRP tracks the availability of interface FastEthernet 0/1. If FastEthernet 0/1 goes down, the priority of the switch in group 1 is decremented by 20.
DLS1(config-if)#`standby 1 track fastEthernet 0/2`	HSRP tracks the availability of interface FastEthernet 0/2. If FastEthernet 0/2 goes down, the priority of the switch in group 1 is decremented by the default value of 10.
DLS1(config-if)#`exit`	Moves to global configuration mode.
DLS1(config)#`interface vlan 10`	Moves to interface configuration mode.
DLS1(config-if)#`standby 10 ip 192.168.10.254`	Activates HSRP group 10 on the interface and creates a virtual IP address of 192.168.10.254 for use in HSRP.
DLS1(config-if)#`standby 10 priority 105`	Assigns a priority value of 105 to standby group 1.
DLS1(config-if)#`standby 10 preempt`	Preempts, or takes control of, VLAN 10 forwarding if the local priority is higher than the active switch VLAN 10 priority.

`DLS1(config-if)#standby 10 track fastEthernet 0/1 20`	HSRP tracks the availability of interface FastEthernet 0/1. If FastEthernet 0/1 goes down, the priority of the switch in group 10 is decremented by 20.
`DLS1(config-if)#standby 10 track fastEthernet 0/2`	HSRP tracks the availability of interface FastEthernet 0/2. If FastEthernet 0/2 goes down, the priority of the switch in group 10 is decremented by the default value of 10.
`DLS1(config-if)#exit`	Moves to global configuration mode.
`DLS1(config)#interface vlan 20`	Moves to interface configuration mode.
`DLS1(config-if)#standby 20 ip 192.168.20.254`	Activates HSRP group 20 on the interface and creates a virtual IP address of 192.168.20.254 for use in HSRP.
`DLS1(config-if)#standby 20 priority 100`	Assigns a priority value of 100 to standby group 20.
`DLS1(config-if)#standby 20 track fastEthernet 0/1 20`	HSRP tracks the availability of interface FastEthernet 0/1. If FastEthernet 0/1 goes down, the priority of the switch in group 20 is decremented by 20.
`DLS1(config-if)#standby 20 track fastEthernet 0/2`	HSRP tracks the availability of interface FastEthernet 0/2. If FastEthernet 0/2 goes down, the priority of the switch in group 20 is decremented by the default value of 10.
`DLS1(config-if)#exit`	Moves to global configuration mode.
`DLS1(config)#interface vlan 30`	Moves to interface configuration mode.
`DLS1(config-if)#standby 30 ip 192.168.30.254`	Activates HSRP group 30 on the interface and creates a virtual IP address of 192.168.30.254 for use in HSRP.

DLS1(config-if)#**standby 30 priority 100**	Assigns a priority value of 100 to standby group 30.
DLS1(config-if)#**standby 30 track fastEthernet 0/1 20**	HSRP tracks the availability of interface FastEthernet 0/1. If FastEthernet 0/1 goes down, the priority of the switch in group 30 is decremented by 20.
DLS1(config-if)#**standby 30 track fastEthernet 0/2**	HSRP tracks the availability of interface FastEthernet 0/2. If FastEthernet 0/2 goes down, the priority of the switch in group 30 is decremented by the default value of 10.
DLS1(config-if)#**exit**	Moves to global configuration mode.

Switch DLS2

DLS2(config)#**interface vlan 1**	Moves to interface configuration mode.
DLS2(config-if)#**standby 1 ip 192.168.1.254**	Activates HSRP group 1 on the interface and creates a virtual IP address of 192.168.1.254 for use in HSRP.
DLS2(config-if)#**standby 1 priority 100**	Assigns a priority value of 100 to standby group 1.
DLS2(config-if)#**standby 1 track fastEthernet 0/1 20**	HSRP tracks the availability of interface FastEthernet 0/1. If FastEthernet 0/1 goes down, the priority of the switch in group 1 is decremented by 20.
DLS2(config-if)#**standby 1 track fastEthernet 0/2**	HSRP tracks the availability of interface FastEthernet 0/2. If FastEthernet 0/2 goes down, the priority of the switch in group 1 is decremented by the default value of 10.
DLS2(config-if)#**exit**	Moves to global configuration mode.
DLS2(config)#**interface vlan 10**	Moves to interface configuration mode.

`DLS2(config-if)#standby 10 ip 192.168.10.254`	Activates HSRP group 10 on the interface and creates a virtual IP address of 192.168.10.254 for use in HSRP.
`DLS2(config-if)#standby 10 priority 100`	Assigns a priority value of 100 to standby group 10.
`DLS2(config-if)#standby 10 track fastEthernet 0/1 20`	HSRP tracks the availability of interface FastEthernet 0/1. If FastEthernet 0/1 goes down, the priority of the switch in group 10 is decremented by 20.
`DLS2(config-if)#standby 10 track fastEthernet 0/2`	HSRP tracks the availability of interface FastEthernet 0/2. If FastEthernet 0/2 goes down, the priority of the switch in group 10 is decremented by the default value of 10.
`DLS2(config-if)#exit`	Moves to global configuration mode.
`DLS2(config)#interface vlan 20`	Moves to interface configuration mode.
`DLS2(config-if)#standby 20 ip 192.168.20.254`	Activates HSRP group 20 on the interface and creates a virtual IP address of 192.168.20.254 for use in HSRP.
`DLS2(config-if)#standby 20 priority 105`	Assigns a priority value of 105 to standby group 20.
`DLS2(config-if)#standby 20 preempt`	Preempts, or takes control of, VLAN 20 forwarding if the local priority is higher than the active switch VLAN 20 priority.
`DLS2(config-if)#standby 20 track fastEthernet 0/1 20`	HSRP tracks the availability of interface FastEthernet 0/1. If FastEthernet 0/1 goes down, the priority of the switch in group 20 is decremented by 20.
`DLS2(config-if)#standby 20 track fastEthernet 0/2`	HSRP tracks the availability of interface FastEthernet 0/2. If FastEthernet 0/2 goes down, the priority of the switch in group 20 is decremented by the default value of 10.

DLS2(config-if)#**exit**	Moves to global configuration mode.
DLS2(config)#**interface vlan 30**	Moves to interface configuration mode.
DLS2(config-if)#**standby 30 ip 192.168.30.254**	Activates HSRP group 30 on the interface and creates a virtual IP address of 192.168.30.254 for use in HSRP.
DLS2(config-if)#**standby 30 priority 105**	Assigns a priority value of 105 to standby group 30.
DLS2(config-if)#**standby 30 preempt**	Preempts, or takes control of, VLAN 30 forwarding if the local priority is higher than the active switch VLAN 30 priority.
DLS2(config-if)#**standby 30 track fastEthernet 0/1 20**	HSRP tracks the availability of interface FastEthernet 0/1. If FastEthernet 0/1 goes down, the priority of the switch in group 30 is decremented by 20.
DLS2(config-if)#**standby 30 track fastEthernet 0/2**	HSRP tracks the availability of interface FastEthernet 0/2. If FastEthernet 0/2 goes down, the priority of the switch in group 30 is decremented by the default value of 10.
DLS2(config-if)#**exit**	Moves to global configuration mode.

IP SLA Tracking—Switch DLS1 VLAN 10

DLS1(config)#**ip sla 10**	Creates SLA process 10.
DLS1(config-ip-sla)#**icmp-echo 192.168.10.1**	Configures the SLA as an ICMP Echo operation to destination 192.168.10.1.
DLS1(config-ip-sla-echo)#**exit**	Exits SLA configuration mode.
DLS1(config)#**ip sla schedule 10 start-time now life forever**	Configures the scheduling for SLA 10 process to start now and continue indefinitely.
DLS1(config)#**track 90 ip sla 10 state**	Creates an object, 90, to track the state of SLA process 10.

`DLS1(config-track)#`**`exit`**	Moves to global configuration mode.
`DLS1(config)#`**`interface vlan 10`**	Moves to interface configuration mode.
`DLS1(config-if)#`**`standby 10 track 90`** **`decrement 20`**	Tracks the state of object 90 and decrements the device priority by 20 if the object fails.
`DLS1(config-if)#`**`exit`**	Moves to global configuration mode.

Configuration Example: GLBP

Figure 6-3 shows the network topology for the configuration that follows, which shows how to configure GLBP using commands covered in this chapter. Note that the example shows only the commands specific to GLBP.

> **NOTE:** The Gateway Load Balancing Protocol (GLBP) is not supported on the Catalyst 3750-E, 3750, 3560, or 3550 platforms. GLBP is supported on the Catalyst 4500 and Catalyst 6500 platforms.

Figure 6-3   *Network Topology for GLBP Configuration Example*

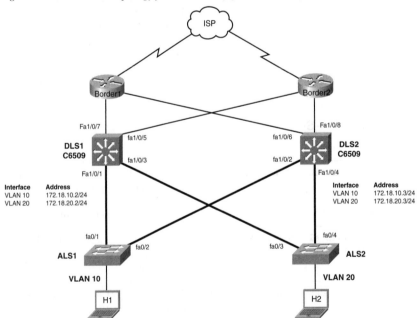

DLS1 and DLS2 belong to GLBP groups 10 and 20. DLS1 is the AVG for GLBP group 10 and backup for GLBP group 20. DLS2 is the AVG for GLBP group 20 and backup for GLBP group 10.

DLS1 and DLS2 are responsible for the virtual IP address 172.18.10.1 on VLAN 10 and 172.18.20.1 on VLAN 20.

DLS1

`DLS1(config)#track 90 interface fastethernet 1/0/7 line-protocol`	Configures tracking object 90 to monitor the line-protocol on interface fastEthernet 1/0/7.
`DLS1(config)#track 91 interface fastethernet 1/0/5 line-protocol`	Configures tracking object 91 to monitor the line-protocol on interface fastEthernet 1/0/5.
`DLS1(config)#interface vlan 10`	Moves to interface configuration mode.
`DLS1(config-if)#ip address 172.18.10.2 255.255.255.0`	Assigns an IP address and netmask.
`DLS1(config-if)#glbp 10 ip 172.18.10.1`	Enables GLBP for group 10 on this interface with a virtual address of 172.18.10.1.
`DLS1(config-if)#glbp 10 weighting 110 lower 95 upper 105`	Specifies the initial weighting value, and the upper and lower thresholds, for a GLBP gateway.
`DLS1(config-if)#glbp 10 timers msec 200 msec 700`	Configures the hello timer to be 200 milliseconds and the hold timer to be 700 milliseconds.
`DLS1(config-if)#glbp 10 priority 105`	Sets the priority level to 105 on the switch for VLAN 10.
`DLS1(config-if)#glbp 10 preempt delay minimum 300`	Configures the switch to take over as AVG for group 10 if this switch has a higher priority than the current active virtual forwarder (AVF) after a delay of 300 seconds.
`DLS1(config-if)#glbp 10 authentication md5 key-string xyz123`	Configures the authentication key *xyz123* for GLBP packets received from the other switch in the group.

DLS1(config-if)#`glbp 10 weighting track 90 decrement 10`	Configures object 90 to be tracked in group 10. Decrements the weight by 10 if the object fails.
DLS1(config-if)#`glbp 10 weighting track 91 decrement 20`	Configures object 91 to be tracked in group 10. Decrements the weight by 20 if the object fails.
DLS1(config)#`interface vlan 20`	Moves to interface configuration mode.
DLS1(config-if)#`ip address 172.18.20.2 255.255.255.0`	Assigns an IP address and netmask.
DLS1(config-if)#`glbp 20 ip 172.18.20.1`	Enables GLBP for group 1 on this interface with a virtual address of 172.18.20.1.
DLS1(config-if)#`glbp 20 weighting 110 lower 95 upper 105`	Specifies the initial weighting value, and the upper and lower thresholds, for a GLBP gateway.
DLS1(config-if)#`glbp 20 timers msec 200 msec 700`	Configures the hello timer to be 200 milliseconds and the hold timer to be 700 milliseconds.
DLS1(config-if)#`glbp 20 priority 100`	Sets the priority level to 100 on the switch for VLAN 20.
DLS1(config-if)#`glbp 20 preempt delay minimum 300`	Configures the switch to take over as AVG for group 10 if this switch has a higher priority than the current active virtual forwarder (AVF) after a delay of 300 seconds.
DLS1(config-if)#`glbp 20 authentication md5 key-string xyz123`	Configures the authentication key *xyz123* for GLBP packets received from the other switch in the group.
DLS1(config-if)#`glbp 20 weighting track 90 decrement 10`	Configures object 90 to be tracked in group 20. Decrements the weight by 10 if the object fails.
DLS1(config-if)#`glbp 20 weighting track 91 decrement 10`	Configures object 91 to be tracked in group 20. Decrements the weight by 10 if the object fails.

DLS2

DLS2(config)#**track 90 interface fastethernet 1/0/8 line-protocol**	Configures tracking object 90 to monitor the line-protocol on interface fastEthernet 1/0/8.
DLS2(config)#**track 91 interface fastethernet 1/0/6 line-protocol**	Configures tracking object 91 to monitor the line-protocol on interface fastEthernet 1/0/6.
DLS2(config)#**interface vlan 10**	Moves to interface configuration mode.
DLS2(config-if)#**ip address 172.18.10.3 255.255.255.0**	Assigns IP address and netmask.
DLS2(config-if)#**glbp 10 ip 172.18.10.1**	Enables GLBP for group 10 on this interface with a virtual address of 172.18.10.1.
DLS2(config-if)#**glbp 10 weighting 110 lower 95 upper 105**	Specifies the initial weighting value, and the upper and lower thresholds, for a GLBP gateway.
DLS2(config-if)#**glbp 10 timers msec 200 msec 700**	Configures the hello timer to be 200 milliseconds and the hold timer to be 700 milliseconds.
DLS2(config-if)#**glbp 10 priority 100**	Sets the priority level to 100 on the switch for VLAN 10.
DLS2(config-if)#**glbp 10 preempt delay minimum 300**	Configures the switch to take over as AVG for group 10 if this switch has a higher priority than the current active virtual forwarder (AVF) after a delay of 300 seconds.
DLS2(config-if)#**glbp 10 authentication md5 key-string xyz123**	Configures the authentication key xyz123 for GLBP packets received from the other switch in the group.
DLS2(config-if)#**glbp 10 weighting track 90 decrement 10**	Configures object 90 to be tracked in group 10. Decrements the weight by 10 if the object fails.
DLS2(config-if)#**glbp 10 weighting track 91 decrement 20**	Configures object 91 to be tracked in group 10. Decrements the weight by 20 if the object fails.
DLS2(config)#**interface vlan 20**	Moves to interface configuration mode.

DLS2(config-if)#ip address 172.18.20.3 255.255.255.0	Assigns IP address and netmask.
DLS2(config-if)#glbp 20 ip 172.18.20.1	Enables GLBP for group 1 on this interface with a virtual address of 172.18.20.1.
DLS2(config-if)#glbp 20 weighting 110 lower 95 upper 105	Specifies the initial weighting value, and the upper and lower thresholds, for a GLBP gateway.
DLS2(config-if)#glbp 20 timers msec 200 msec 700	Configures the hello timer to be 200 milliseconds and the hold timer to be 700 milliseconds.
DLS2(config-if)#glbp 20 priority 105	Sets the priority level to 105 on the switch for VLAN 20.
DLS2(config-if)#glbp 20 preempt delay minimum 300	Configures the switch to take over as AVG for group 10 if this switch has a higher priority than the current active virtual forwarder (AVF) after a delay of 300 seconds.
DLS2(config-if)#glbp 20 authentication md5 key-string xyz123	Configures the authentication key *xyz123* for GLBP packets received from the other switch in the group.
DLS2(config-if)#glbp 20 weighting track 90 decrement 10	Configures object 90 to be tracked in group 20. Decrements the weight by 10 if the object fails.
DLS2(config-if)#glbp 20 weighting track 91 decrement 10	Configures object 91 to be tracked in group 20. Decrements the weight by 10 if the object fails.

CHAPTER 7

Minimizing Service Loss and Data Theft in a Campus Network

This chapter provides information and commands concerning the following topics:

- Configuring static MAC addresses
- Configuring switch port security
- Programming authentication methods
- Adding 802.1x port-based authentication
- Mitigating VLAN hopping: Best practices
- DHCP snooping
- Implementing Dynamic ARP Inspection (DAI)
- Configuring IP Source Guard
- Understanding Cisco Discovery Protocol (CDP) security issues
- Configuring the Secure Shell (SSH) protocol
- Restricting management access with access control lists (ACLs)
- Disabling unneeded services
- Securing end-device access ports

Configuring Static MAC Addresses

You can define the forwarding behavior of a switch port by adding a static MAC address to your configuration. This MAC address can be either a unicast or a multicast address, and the entry does not age and is retained when the switch restarts.

`Switch(config)#mac address-table static cf23.1943.9a4b vlan 1 interface fastethernet 0/3`	Destination MAC address cf23.1943.9a4b is added to the MAC address table. Packets with this address are forwarded out interface fastethernet 0/3.
	NOTE: Beginning with Cisco IOS Software Release 12.1(11)EA1, the **mac address-table static** command (no hyphen) replaces **the mac-address-table** command (with the hyphen). The **mac-address-table static** command (with the hyphen) becomes obsolete in a future release.

`Switch(config)#mac address-table static 1234.5678.90ab vlan 4 interface gigabitethernet 0/1`	Destination MAC address 1234.5678.90ab is added to the MAC address table. Packets with this address are forwarded out interface gigabitethernet 0/1.

Configuring Switch Port Security

`Switch(config)#interface fastethernet 0/1`	Moves to interface configuration mode.
`Switch(config-if)#switchport port-security`	Enables port security on the interface.
`Switch(config-if)#switchport port-security maximum 4`	Sets a maximum limit of four MAC addresses that are allowed on this port.
	NOTE: The maximum number of secure MAC addresses that you can configure on a switch is set by the maximum number of available MAC addresses allowed in the system.
`Switch(config-if)#switchport port-security mac-address 1234.5678.90ab`	Sets a specific secure MAC address 1234.5678.90ab. You can add additional secure MAC addresses up to the maximum value configured.
`Switch(config-if)#switchport port-security violation shutdown`	Configures port security to shut down the interface if a security violation occurs.
	NOTE: In shutdown mode, the port is errdisabled, a log entry is made, and manual intervention or errdisable recovery must be used to reenable the interface.
`Switch(config-if)#switchport port-security violation restrict`	Configures port security to restrict mode if a security violation occurs.
	NOTE: In restrict mode, frames from a non-allowed address are dropped and a log entry is made. The interface remains operational.

`Switch(config-if)#`**`switchport port-security violation protect`**	Configures port security to protect mode if a security violation occurs.
	NOTE: In protect mode, frames from a non-allowed address are dropped but no log entry is made. The interface remains operational.

Verifying Switch Port Security

`Switch#`**`show port-security`**	Displays security information for all interfaces.
`Switch#`**`show port-security interface fastethernet 0/5`**	Displays security information for interface fastethernet 0/5.
`Switch#`**`show port-security address`**	Displays MAC address table security Information.
`Switch#`**`show mac address-table`**	Displays the MAC address table.
`Switch#`**`clear mac address-table dynamic`**	Deletes all dynamic MAC addresses.
`Switch#`**`clear mac address-table dynamic address aaaa.bbbb.cccc`**	Deletes the specified dynamic MAC address.
`Switch#`**`clear mac address-table dynamic interface fastethernet 0/5`**	Deletes all dynamic MAC addresses on interface FastEthernet 0/5.
`Switch#`**`clear mac address-table dynamic vlan 10`**	Deletes all dynamic MAC addresses on VLAN 10.
`Switch#`**`clear mac address-table notification`**	Clears MAC notification global counters.
	NOTE: Beginning with Cisco IOS Software Release 12.1(11)EA1, the **clear mac address-table** command (no hyphen) replaces the **clear mac-address-table** command (with the hyphen). The **clear mac-address-table static** command (with the hyphen) becomes obsolete in a future release.

Sticky MAC Addresses

Sticky MAC addresses are a feature of port security. Sticky MAC addresses limit switch port access to a specific MAC address that can be dynamically learned, as opposed to a network administrator manually associating a MAC address with a specific switch port. These addresses are stored in the running configuration file. If this file is saved, the sticky MAC addresses will not have to be relearned when the switch is rebooted, providing a high level of switch port security.

`Switch(config)#interface fastethernet 0/5`	Moves to interface config mode.
`Switch(config-if)#switchport port-security mac-address sticky`	Converts all dynamic port security-learned MAC addresses to sticky secure MAC addresses.
`Switch(config-if)#switchport port-security mac-address sticky vlan 10 voice`	Converts all dynamic port security-learned MAC addresses to sticky secure MAC addresses on voice VLAN 10.
	NOTE: The **voice** keyword is available only if a voice VLAN is first configured on a port and if that port is not the access VLAN.

Programming Authentication Methods

`Switch(config)#username admin secret cisco`	Creates a user with username *admin* and encrypted password *cisco*.
`Switch(config)#radius-server host 192.168.55.12 auth-port 1812 key S3CR3TKEY`	Specifies a RADIUS server at 192.168.55.12 with S3CR3TKEY as the authentication key using UDP port 1812 for authentication requests.
`Switch(config)#aaa new-model`	Enables the authentication, authorization, and accounting (AAA) access control mode.
`Switch(config)#aaa authentication login default group radius local line`	Sets login authentication for the default user group. Authenticates to the RADIUS server first and locally defined users second, and uses the line password as the last resort.
`Switch(config)#aaa authentication login NO_AUTH none`	Specifies the authentication method NO_AUTH to require no authentication.
`Switch(config)#line vty 0 15`	Enters VTY configuration mode.

`Switch(config-line)#login authentication default`	Uses the IOS AAA service to authenticate the default user group.
`Switch(config-line)#password S3cr3Tw0Rd`	Specifies a password on lines 0 through 15.
`Switch(config-line)#line console 0`	Enters console 0 configuration mode.
`Switch(config-line)#login authentication NO_AUTH`	Specifies the AAA service to use the authentication method NO_AUTH when a user logs in.
	NOTE: If authentication is not specifically set for a line, the default is to deny access and no authentication is performed.

Adding 802.1x Port-Based Authentication

The IEEE 802.1x standard defines an access control and authentication protocol that prevents unauthorized hosts from connecting to a LAN through publicly accessible ports unless they are properly authenticated. The authentication server authenticates each host connected to a switch port before making available any services offered by the switch or the LAN.

`Switch(config)#aaa new-model`	Enables authentication, authorization, and accounting (AAA).
`Switch(config)#aaa authentication dot1x default group radius`	Creates an 802.1x port-based authentication method list. This method specifies using a RADIUS server for authentication.
	NOTE: A method list describes the sequence and authentication methods to be queried to authenticate a user. The software uses the first method listed to authenticate users; if that method fails to respond, the software selects the next authentication method in the method list. This process continues until there is successful communication with a listed authentication method or until all defined methods are exhausted. If authentication fails at any point in this cycle, the authentication process stops, and no other authentication methods are attempted.
	NOTE: To create a default list that is used when a named list is not specified, use the **default** keyword followed by methods that are to be used in default situations.

	NOTE: When using the **aaa authentication dot1x** command, you must use at least one of the following keywords: **group radius**—Uses a list of RADIUS servers for authentication. **none**—Uses no authentication. The client is automatically authenticated without the switch using information supplied by the client. This method should only be used as a second method. If the first method of **group radius** is not successful, the switch uses the second method for authentication until a method is successful. In this case, no authentication is used.
`Switch(config)#dot1x system-auth-control`	Globally enables 802.1x port-based authentication.
`Switch(config)#interface fastethernet 0/1`	Moves to interface config mode.
`Switch(config-if)# authentication port-control auto`	Enables 802.1x authentication on this interface.
	NOTE: The **authentication port-control** command supercedes the **dot1x port-control** command in IOS version 12.2(50)SE. Both commands are supported.
	NOTE: The **auto** keyword enables the port to begin in the unauthorized state. This enables only Extensible Authentication Protocol over LAN (EAPOL) frames to be sent and received through the port. The following are other available keywords: **force-authorized**—Disables 802.1x authentication and causes the port to transition to the authorized state without any authentication exchange required. This is the default setting. **force-unauthorized**—Causes the port to remain in the unauthorized state, ignoring all attempts by the client to authenticate. The switch cannot provide authentication services to the client through the interface.
`Switch#show dot1x`	Verifies your 802.1x entries.

Mitigating VLAN Hopping: Best Practices

Configure all unused ports as access ports so that trunking cannot be negotiated across those links.

Place all unused ports in the shutdown state and associate with a VLAN designed only for unused ports, carrying no user data traffic.

When establishing a trunk link, purposefully configure the following:

- The native VLAN to be different from any data VLANs
- Trunking as on rather than negotiated
- The specific VLAN range to be carried on the trunk

VLAN Access Maps

VLAN access maps are the only way to control filtering within a VLAN. VLAN access maps have no direction—if you want to filter traffic in a specific direction, you must include an access control list (ACL) with specific source or destination addresses. VLAN access maps do not work on the 2960 platform, but they do work on the 3560, 3750, and the 6500 platforms.

`Switch(config)#ip access-list extended TEST1`	Creates a named extended ACL called TEST1.
`Switch(config-ext-nacl)#permit tcp any any`	The first line of an extended ACL permits any TCP packet from any source to travel to any destination address. Because there is no other line in this ACL, the implicit **deny** statement that is part of all ACLS deny any other packet.
`Switch(config-ext-nacl)#exit`	Exits named ACL configuration mode and returns to global config mode.
`Switch(config)#mac access-list extended SERVER2`	Creates the extended MAC access-list SERVER2.
`Switch(config-ext-macl)#permit any host 0000.1111.2222`	Permits traffic from any source to the destination specified by the MAC address 0000.1111.2222.
	NOTE: Because the access-list is called in the access-map DROP1, the **permit** statement in the MAC access-list does not permit this traffic but rather chooses the traffic that will be acted upon in the action portion of the access-map.

`Switch(config)#`**`vlan access-map`** **`DROP1 5`**	Creates a VLAN access map named DROP1 and moves into VLAN access map configuration mode. A sequence number of 5 is assigned to this access map. If no sequence number is given at the end of the command, a default number of 10 is assigned.
`Switch(config-access-map)#`**`match`** **`ip address TEST1`**	Defines what needs to occur for this action to continue. In this case, packets filtered out by the named ACL test1 will be acted upon.
	NOTE: You can match ACLs based on the following: IP ACL number: 1–199 and 1300–2699 IP ACL name IPX ACL number: 800–999 IPX ACL name MAC address ACL name
`Switch(config-access-map)#`**`action drop`**	Any packet that is filtered out by the ACL test1 will be dropped.
	NOTE: You can configure the following actions: Drop Forward Redirect (works only on a Catalyst 6500)
`Switch(config)#`**`vlan access-map`** **`DROP1 10`**	Creates line 10 of the VLAN access map named DROP1.
`Switch(config-map)#`**`match mac`** **`address SERVER2`**	Matches the MAC access list filter SERVER2.
`Switch(config-map)#`**`action drop`**	Drops all traffic permitted by the MAC access-list SERVER2.

Switch(config-map)#**vlan access-map DROP1 15**	Creates line 15 of the VLAN access map named DROP1.
Switch(config-map)#**action forward**	Forwards traffic not specified to be dropped in line 5 and 10 of the VLAN access-map DROP1.
Switch(config-map)#**exit**	Exits access-map configuration mode.
Switch(config)#**vlan filter DROP1 vlan-list 20-30**	Applies the VLAN map named DROP1 to VLANs 20–30.
	NOTE: The **vlan-list** argument can refer to a single VLAN (26), a consecutive list (20–30), or a string of VLAN IDs (12, 22, 32). Spaces around the comma and hyphen are optional.

Verifying VLAN Access Maps

Switch#**show vlan access-map**	Displays all VLAN access maps.
Switch#**show vlan access-map DROP1**	Displays the VLAN access map named DROP1.
Switch#**show vlan filter**	Displays what filters are applied to all VLANs.
Switch#**show vlan filter access-map DROP1**	Displays the filter for the specific VLAN access map named DROP1.

Configuration Example: VLAN Access Maps

Figure 7-1 shows the network topology for the configuration that follows, which shows how to configure VLAN access maps using the commands covered in this chapter.

Figure 7-1   Network Topology for VLAN Access Map Configuration

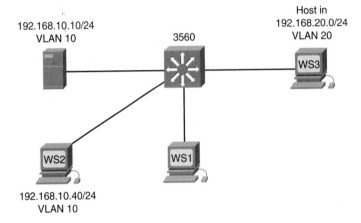

The objective of the VLAN access map is to deny all IP traffic from VLAN 20 from reaching the server in VLAN 10. A specific host in VLAN 10 with an IP address of 192.168.10.40/24 is also denied access to the server. All other IP traffic is allowed. A 3560 switch is used for this example.

`3560(config)#ip access-list extended DENY_SERVER_ACL`	Creates a named ACL called DENY_SERVER_ACL and moves to named ACL configuration mode.
`3560(config-ext-nacl)#permit ip 192.168.20.0 0.0.0.255 host 192.168.10.10`	Filters out all IP packets from a source address of 192.168.20.*x* destined for the server at 192.168.10.10.

3560(config-ext-nacl)#**permit ip host 192.168.10.40 host 192.168.10.10**	Filters out all IP packets from a source address of 192.168.10.40 destined for the server at 192.168.10.10.
3560(config-ext-nacl)#**exit**	Returns to global config mode.
3560(config)#**vlan access-map DENY_SERVER_MAP 10**	Creates a VLAN access map called DENY_SERVER_MAP and moves into VLAN access map config mode. If no sequence number is given at the end of the command, a default number of 10 is assigned.
3560(config-access-map)#**match ip address DENY_SERVER_ACL**	Defines what needs to occur for this action to continue. In this case, packets filtered out by the named ACL DENY_SERVER_ACL are acted upon.
3560(config-access-map)#**action drop**	Any packet filtered out by the ACL is dropped.
3560(config-access-map)#**exit**	Returns to global config mode.
3560(config)#**vlan access-map DENY_SERVER_MAP 20**	Creates line 20 of the VLAN access map called DENY_SERVER_MAP and moves into VLAN access map config mode.
3560(config-access-map)#**action forward**	Any packet not filtered out by the ACL in line 10 is forwarded.
3560(config-access-map)#**exit**	Returns to global config mode.
3560(config)#**vlan filter DENY_SERVER_MAP vlan-list 10**	Applies the VLAN map to VLAN 10.

DHCP Snooping

DHCP snooping is a DHCP security feature that provides network security by filtering untrusted DHCP messages and by building and maintaining a DHCP snooping binding database, which is also referred to as a DHCP snooping binding table.

Switch(config)#**ip dhcp snooping**	Enables DHCP snooping globally.

	NOTE: If you enable DHCP snooping on a switch, the following DHCP relay agent commands are not available until snooping is disabled:
	
	`Switch(config)#ip dhcp relay information check`
	
	`Switch(config)#ip dhcp relay information policy {drop | keep | replace}Switch(config)#ip dhcp relay information trust-all`
	
	`Switch(config-if)#ip dhcp relay information trusted`
	
	If you enter these commands with DHCP snooping enabled, the switch returns an error message.

`Switch(config)#ip dhcp snooping vlan 20`	Enables DHCP snooping on VLAN 20.
`Switch(config)#ip dhcp snooping vlan 10-35`	Enables DHCP snooping on VLANs 10–35.
`Switch(config)#ip dhcp snooping vlan 20 30`	Enables DHCP snooping on VLANs 20–30.
`Switch(config)#ip dhcp snooping vlan 10,12,14`	Enables DHCP snooping on VLANs 10, 12, and 14.
`Switch(config)#ip dhcp snooping information option`	Enables DHCP option 82 insertion.
	NOTE: DHCP address allocation is usually based on an IP address—either the gateway IP address or the incoming interface IP address. In some networks, you might need additional information to determine which IP address to allocate. By using the relay agent information option—option 82—the Cisco IOS relay agent can include additional information about itself when forwarding DHCP packets to a DHCP server. The relay agent adds the circuit identifier suboption and the remote ID suboption to the relay information option and forwards this all to the DHCP server.

Switch(config)#**interface fasthethernet 0/1**	Moves to interface config mode.
Switch(config-if)#**switchport trunk encapsulation dot1q**	Creates an uplink trunk with 802.1q encapsulation.
Switch(config-if)#**switchport mode trunk**	Forces the switchport to be a trunk.
Switch(config-if)#**switchport trunk allowed vlan 10,20**	Selects VLANs that are allowed transport on the trunk.
Switch(config-if)#**ip dhcp snooping trust**	Configures the interface as trusted.
	NOTE: There must be at least one trusted interface when working with DHCP snooping. It is usually the port connected to the DHCP server or to uplink ports. By default, all ports are untrusted.
Switch(config-if)#**ip dhcp snooping limit rate 75**	Configures the number of DHCP packets per second that an interface can receive.
	NOTE: The range of packets that can be received per second is 1 to 4,294,967,294. The default is no rate configured.
	TIP: Cisco recommends an untrusted rate limit of no more than 100 packets per second.
Switch(config-if)#**ip dhcp snooping verify mac-address**	Configures the switch to verify that the source MAC address in a DHCP packet that is received on an untrusted port matches the client hardware address in the packet.

Verifying DHCP Snooping

Switch#**show ip dhcp snooping**	Displays the DHCP snooping configuration for a switch.
Switch#**show ip dhcp snooping binding**	Displays only the dynamically configured bindings in the DHCP snooping binding database.
Switch#**show running-config**	Displays the status of the insertion and removal of the DHCP option 82 field on all interfaces.

Implementing Dynamic ARP Inspection

Dynamic ARP Inspection (DAI) determines the validity of an ARP packet. This feature prevents attacks on the switch by not relaying invalid ARP requests and responses to other ports in the same VLAN. DAI does not work on the 2960.

> **NOTE:**   To use this feature, you must have the enhanced multilayer image (EMI) installed on your 3560 switch.

`3560Switch(config)#ip arp inspection vlan 10`	Enables DAI on VLAN 10.
`3560Switch(config)#ip arp inspection vlan 10,20`	Enables DAI on VLANs 10 and 20.
`3560Switch(config)#ip arp inspection vlan 10-20`	Enables DAI on VLANs 10 to 20 inclusive.
`3560Switch(config)#ip arp inspection validate src-mac`	Configures DAI to drop ARP packets when the source MAC address in the body of the ARP packet does not match the source MAC address specified in the Ethernet header. This check is performed on both APR requests and responses.
`3560Switch(config)#ip arp inspection validate dst-mac`	Configures DAI to drop ARP packets when the destination MAC address in the body of the ARP packet does not match the destination MAC address specified in the Ethernet header. This check is performed on both APR requests and responses.
`3560Switch(config)#ip arp inspection validate ip`	Configures DAI to drop ARP packets that have invalid and unexpected IP addresses in the ARP body, such as 0.0.0.0, 255.255.255.255, or all IP multicast addresses. Sender IP addresses are checked in all ARP requests and responses, and target IP addresses are checked only in ARP responses.
`Switch(config)#interface fastethernet 0/24`	Moves to interface config mode.
`Switch(config-if)#ip arp inspection trust`	Configures the connection between switches as trusted.
	NOTE: By default, all interfaces are untrusted.

Verifying DAI

Switch#**show ip arp inspection interfaces**	Verifies the dynamic ARP configuration.
Switch#**show ip arp inspection vlan 10**	Verifies the dynamic ARP configuration for VLAN 10.
Switch#**show ip arp inspection statistics vlan 10**	Displays the dynamic ARP inspection statistics for VLAN 10.

Configuring IP Source Guard

IP Source Guard prevents a malicious host from hijacking its neighbor's IP address. IP Source Guard dynamically maintains a per-port table with IP-to-MAC-to-switch port bindings. This is usually accomplished with the accumulated DHCP Snooping data. The binding table can also be manually populated.

Switch(config)#**ip dhcp snooping**	Enables DHCP snooping globally.
witch(config)#**ip dhcp snooping vlan number 10-35**	Enables DHCP snooping on VLANs 10–35.
Switch(config-if)#**ip verify source**	Enables IP Source Guard with IP address filtering on the port.
Switch(config-if)#**ip verify source port-security**	Enables IP Source Guard with IP and MAC address filtering on the port.
Switch(config)#**exit**	Exits interface configuration mode.
Switch(config)# **ip source binding 0000.1111.2222 vlan 35 10.1.1.1 interface gigabitethernet1/0/1**	Adds a static IP source binding between MAC 0000.1111.2222, VLAN 35, address 10.1.1.1, and interface gigabitethernet1/0/1.
Switch#**show ip source binding**	Displays the IP source bindings on a switch.
Switch#**show ip verify source**	Displays the IP Source Guard configuration on the switch or on a specific interface.
	NOTE: IP Source Guard is not supported on EtherChannels.

Understanding Cisco Discovery Protocol Security Issues

Although Cisco Discovery Protocol (CDP) is necessary for some management applications, CDP should still be disabled in some instances.

Disable CDP globally under these scenarios:

- CDP is not required at all.
- The device is located in an insecure environment.

Use the command **no cdp run** to disable CDP globally:

```
Switch(config)#no cdp run
```

Disable CDP on any interface under these scenarios:

- Management is not being performed.
- The interface is a nontrunk interface.
- The interface is connected to a nontrusted network.

Use the interface configuration command **no cdp enable** to disable CDP on a specific interface:

```
Switch(config)#interface fastethernet 0/12
Switch(config-if)#no cdp enable
```

Link Layer Discovery Protocol Configuration

IEEE 802.1AB Link Layer Discovery Protocol (LLDP) is a neighbor discovery protocol that is used for network devices to advertise information about themselves to other devices on the network.

Switch(config)#**lldp run**	Enables LLDP globally.
Switch(config)#**lldp holdtime 120**	Specifies how long a receiving device should hold your device information before discarding it.
Switch(config)#**lldp reinit 2**	Configures the delay time (seconds) for LLDP to initialize on an interface.
Switch(config)#**lldp timer 30**	Sets the sending frequency of LLDP updates in seconds.
Switch(config)#**interface fastethernet 0/0**	Moves to interface configuration mode.
Switch(config-if)#**lldp transmit**	Enables the interface to send LLDP packets.

`Switch(config-if)#lldp receive`	Enables the interface to receive LLDP packets.
`Switch#show lldp interface`	Displays information about interfaces where LLDP is enabled.
`Switch#show lldp interface fastethernet 0/10`	Limits display information about LLDP to interface fastethernet 0/10.
`Switch#show lldp neighbors detail`	Displays neighbor device type, interface type and number, holdtime, capabilities, and port ID.

Configuring the Secure Shell Protocol

CAUTION: Secure Shell (SSH) version 1 implementations have known security issues. It is recommended to use SSH version 2 whenever possible.

NOTE: To work, SSH requires a local username database, a local IP domain, and an RSA key to be generated.

The Cisco implementation of SSH requires Cisco IOS Software to support Rivest, Shamir, Adleman (RSA) authentication, and minimum Data Encryption Standard (DES) encryption—a cryptographic software image.

`Switch(config)#username Roland password tower`	Creates a locally significant username/password combination. These are the credentials needed to be entered when connecting to the switch with SSH client software.
`Switch(config)#ip domain-name test.lab`	Creates a host domain for the switch.
`Switch(config)#crypto key generate rsa`	Enables the SSH server for local and remote authentication on the switch and generates an RSA key pair.
`Switch(config)#ip ssh version 2`	Configures the switch to run SSH version 2 (SSHv2).
`Switch(config)#line vty 0 15`	Moves to VTY configuration mode.

`Switch(config-line)#`**`login local`**	Authenticates the VTY lines to the local user database.
`Switch(config-line)#`**`transport input ssh`**	Configures SSH communication protocol.
`Switch#`**`show ip ssh`**	Displays whether SSH server is enabled, and version and configuration information.
`Switch#`**`show ssh`**	Shows the status of the SSH server.

Restricting Management Access with ACLs

Telnet Sessions

`Switch(config)#`**`access-list 10 permit host 192.168.1.15`**	Creates a standard ACL that filters out traffic from source address 192.168.1.15.
`Switch(config)#`**`line vty 0 15`**	Moves to VTY line mode. All commands in this mode apply to VTY lines 0–15 inclusive.
`Switch(config-line)#`**`access-class 10 in`**	Restricts incoming VTY connections to addresses filtered by ACL 10.
	NOTE: The actual number of VTY lines depends on the platform and the version of Cisco IOS Software run.

Web Interface Sessions

`Switch(config)#`**`access-list 10 permit host 192.168.1.15`**	Creates a standard ACL that filters out traffic from source address 192.168.1.15.
`Switch(config)#`**`ip http server`**	Enables the HTTP server on the switch.
`Switch(config)#`**`ip http secure-server`**	Enables the HTTPS server on the switch.
`Switch(config)#`**`ip http access-class 10`**	Applies ACL 10 to the HTTP or HTTPS server.
`Switch(config)#`**`ip http authentication local`**	Authenticates HTTP sessions with the router using the local user database.
`Switch(config)#`**`ip http authentication aaa`**	Authenticates HTTP sessions using the router AAA service.

Disabling Unneeded Services

TIP: Cisco devices implement various TCP and User Datagram Protocol (UDP) servers to help facilitate management and integration of devices. If these servers are not needed, consider disabling them to reduce security vulnerabilities.

`Switch(config)#`**`no service tcp-`** **`small-servers`**	Disables minor TCP services—echo, discard, chargen, and daytime—available from hosts on the network.
`Switch(config)#`**`no service udp-`** **`small-servers`**	Disables minor UDP services—echo, discard, and chargen—available from hosts on the network.
`Switch(config)#`**`no ip finger`**	Disables the finger service. The finger service enables remote users to view the output equivalent to the **show users** [**wide**] command.
	NOTE: The previous version of the [**no**] **ip finger** command was the [**no**] **service finger** command. The [**no**] **service finger** command continues to work to maintain backward compatibility, but support for this command might be removed in some future Cisco IOS release.
`Switch(config)#`**`no service`** **`config`**	Disables the config service. The config service enables the autoloading of configuration files from a network server.
`Switch(config)#`**`no ip http`** **`server`**	Disables the HTTP server service.

Securing End-Device Access Ports

`Switch(config)#`**`interface range`** **`fastethernet 0/1 - 24`**	Enters interface range command mode. All commands entered in this mode are applied to all interfaces in the range.
`Switch(config-if-range)#`**`switchport`** **`host`**	Enables the switchport host macro.

NOTE: The **switchport host** command is a macro that performs the following actions:

- Sets the switch port mode to access
- Enables Spanning Tree PortFast
- Disables channel grouping

The **switchport host** command does not have a **no** keyword to disable it. To return an interface to default configuration, use the global configuration command **default interface** *interface-id*:

```
Switch(config)#default interface fasthethernet 0/1
```

CHAPTER 8

Accommodating Voice and Video in Campus Networks

This chapter provides information and commands concerning the following topics:

- Communications subsystems
- Configuring and Verifying Voice VLANs
- Power over Ethernet (PoE)
- High Availability for Voice and Video
- Configuring AutoQoS: 2960/3560/3750
  — Verifying AutoQoS information: 2960/3560/3750
- Configuring AutoQoS: 6500
  — Verifying AutoQoS information: 6500

Figure 8-1 shows the network diagram to be used as a reference for the topics covered in this chapter.

Figure 8-1   Router Switch and Phone

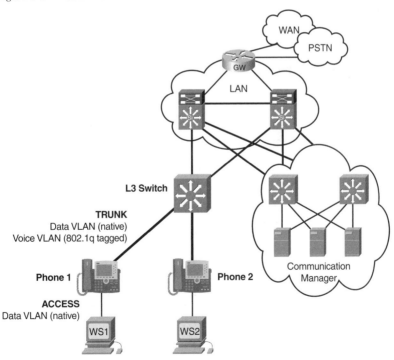

Communications Subsystems

There are four main voice-specific components of the IP telephony network.

IP phones perform voice-to-IP (and vice versa) coding and compression using special hardware. They are active devices requiring power and offer services such as user directory lookups.

Switches provide aggregation and centralized 48Vdc power for the end voice devices using 802.3af PoE inline power. The switches also perform basic quality of service (QoS) functions.

A call-processing manager, such as Cisco Unified Communication Manager, provides the core functionality for call setup and call routing. It also provides scalability and availability using clustering and distributed processing.

A router or switch voice gateway routes voice packets as well as providing backup call functions, access to the traditional telephone networks, and voice coding and translation. Link efficiency mechanisms, such as compression, can also be implemented at the voice gateway. This chapter focuses on the access aggregation switch.

An auxiliary VLAN is configured at the voice and data aggregation access switch. The auxiliary VLAN provides automatic VLAN configuration for IP telephones. This feature places the VoIP phones in their own VLANs without any end-user intervention. By having the IP phone on their own subnet, administrators can more easily identify and troubleshoot as well as create and enforce QoS or security policies. The multi-VLAN access ports are not trunk ports, even though the hardware is set to the dot1q trunk.

Configuring and Verifying Voice VLANs

`Switch(config)#`**`interface`** **`fastethernet 0/1`**	Moves to interface configuration mode.
`Switch(config-if)#`**`switchport mode`** **`access`**	Configures the port to be an access port only.
`Switch(config-if)#`**`switchport access`** **`vlan 10`**	Assigns this port to be a member port in data VLAN 10.
`Switch(config-if)#`**`switchport voice`** **`vlan 110`**	Assigns this port to be a member port in the auxiliary voice VLAN 110.
`Switch(config-if)#`**`spanning-tree`** **`portfast`**	Configures the port to start forwarding data immediately while determining spanning-tree status.

`Switch(config-if)#`**`spanning-tree`** **`bpduguard enable`**	Puts this interface in the error-disabled state if it receives a bridge protocol data unit (BPDU) from another switch.
	NOTE: The BPDU Guard feature can be enabled when the switch is operating in the per-VLAN spanning-tree plus (PVST+), rapid-PVST+, or the multiple spanning-tree (MST) mode.
`Switch(config-if)#`**`cdp enable`**	Enables Cisco Discovery Protocol (CDP) at the interface.
	NOTE: The switch uses the CDP to detect the presence or absence of a Cisco IP Phone. When a Cisco IP Phone is detected, the ingress classification on the port is set to trust the QoS label received in the packet. If the telephone is not detected, the trusted QoS boundary setting on the switch or routed port is disabled and so prevents the misuse of any high-priority queuing.
`Switch#`**`show vlan`**	Displays the VLANs created on the switch and the switch ports assigned to them.

Power over Ethernet

The two common Power over Ethernet (PoE) methods are the Cisco inline power method and the IEEE 802.3af standard. New Cisco devices support both methods for backward compatibility. No specific configuration is required to choose the Cisco pre-standard or the 802.3af standard. Power over Ethernet device detection is enabled through CDP when using a Cisco inline power network device.

NOTE: The new 802.3at amendment of the PoE standard was approved in September 2009. It is rated to supply 25 watts of power at each port. Cisco's pre-standard interim solution, Enhanced PoE, provided 20 watts of power per port. This enhanced capability is available on the C3560E and C3750E LAN switches. Every switch has a dedicated maximum amount of power available for PoE. The power used by each PoE port is deducted from the total available power.

`Switch(config)#interface fastethernet 0/10`	Moves into interface configuration mode.
`Switch(config-if)#power inline auto`	Enables powered-device detection. If enough power is available, automatically allocates power to the PoE port after device detection.
`Switch(config-if)#power inline auto max 10000`	Limits the power to the detected device to 10000 milliwatts (10 watts).
	NOTE: The powered device sends CDP messages to a PoE switch port requesting the amount of power it requires. If the powered device requests more power than the switch port can provide, the PoE port is put in a power-deny state and a system message is generated.
`Switch#show power inline`	Displays the overall PoE budget balance sheet as well as individual port usage and the Cisco device being powered.
`Switch#show power inline fastethernet 0/10`	Displays the PoE status of FastEthernet 0/10.

High Availability for Voice and Video

Typical campus networks are designed with oversubscription because most campus links are underutilized. The rule-of-thumb recommendation for data oversubscription is 20:1 for access ports on the access-to-distribution uplink and 4:1 for the distribution-to-core links. QoS is needed when congestion occurs.

`Switch(config)#mls qos`	Enables quality of service (QoS) for the entire switch.
	NOTE: The switch QoS is disabled by default.
`Switch#show mls qos`	Displays the global QoS configuration.
`Switch(config)#interface fastethernet 0/10`	Moves to interface configuration mode.

`Switch(config-if)#`**`switchport voice`** **`vlan 110`**	Assigns this port to be a member port in the auxiliary voice VLAN 110.
`Switch(config-if)#`**`mls qos trust cos`**	Configures the interface to believe the L2 class of service (CoS) markings on incoming traffic packets. For untagged packets, the default CoS value is used. The default port CoS value is 0.
	NOTE: The **mls qos trust interface** configuration command configures the port trust state. Ingress traffic is trusted, and classification is performed by examining the packet differentiated services code point (DSCP), class of service (CoS), or IP-precedence field. It can also be configured to trust a Cisco IP Phone.
`Switch(config-if)#`**`mls qos trust dscp`**	Configures the interface to believe the L3 differentiated services code point (DSCP) markings on incoming traffic packets. For a non-IP packet, the packet CoS value is used if the packet is tagged. For an untagged packet, the default port CoS value is used.
`Switch(config-if)#`**`mls qos trust ip-`** **`precedence`**	Configures the interface to believe the L3 IP precedence markings on incoming traffic packets. For a non-IP packet, the packet CoS value is used if the packet is tagged. For an untagged packet, the default port CoS value is used.
`Switch(config-if)#`**`mls qos trust`** **`device cisco-phone`**	Configures the switch port to believe the QoS markings of a Cisco IP phone if detected.
`Switch(config-if)#`**`switchport`** **`priority extend cos 0`**	Configures the switch port to send CDP packets to the IP phone instructing the phone as to what CoS markings the phone should add to the data packets that it receives from the device attached to the access port on the Cisco IP Phone. In this case, the CoS value is set to 0.

	NOTE: The CoS value is from 0 to 7, with 7 being the highest priority. The default value is CoS 0.
`Switch(config-if)#switchport priority extend trust`	Sets the priority of data traffic received from the IP Phone access port. The **trust** argument configures the IP Phone access port to trust the priority received from the PC or attached device.
	NOTE: The **mls qos trust extend** command is only valid on the 6500 series switch. Although the 6500 series switch is not tested on the BCMSN certification exam, the **mls qos trust extend** command has been placed in this command guide because of the large number of network professionals working with the 6500 series switch.
	NOTE: With the **mls qos trust extend** command enabled, and if you set your phone to trusted mode, all the packets coming from the PC are sent untouched directly through the phone to the 6500 series switch. If you set the phone to untrusted mode, all traffic coming from the PC are re-marked with the configured CoS value before being sent to the 6500 series switch.
	NOTE: Each time you enter the **mls qos trust extend** command, the mode is changed. If the mode was set to trusted, the result of this command is to change the mode to untrusted. Use the **show queueing interface** command to display the current trust mode.
`Switch#show interfaces fastethernet 0/10 switchport`	Displays the administrative and operational status of the switching port FastEthernet 0/10. This includes port blocking and port protection settings.
`Switch#show mls qos interface fastethernet 0/10`	Shows port-level QoS information for FastEthernet 0/10. This includes trust state and default CoS value.

CAUTION: Although the QoS mechanisms for voice and video are the same, great care must be taken due to the high bandwidth requirements typical to video. This is true for both a one-way video session or an interactive two-way video session.

Configuring AutoQoS: 2960/3560/3750

Auto QoS automatically configures quality of service for voice over IP within a QoS domain. It is disabled by default on all ports. When AutoQoS is enabled on a port, it uses the label on the incoming packet to categorize traffic, to assign other packet labels, and to configure input and output queues. When AutoQoS is used, configure all network devices in a QoS domain with AutoQoS to maintain consistent QoS next hop behavior.

NOTE: The switch applies the auto-QoS–generated commands as if the commands were entered sequentially from the command-line interface (CLI). An existing user configuration can cause the application of the generated commands to fail or to be overridden by the generated commands.

TIP: QoS is globally enabled when AutoQoS is enabled on the first interface.

`Switch(config)#`**`interface fastethernet 0/11`**	Moves to interface configuration mode.
`Switch(config-if)#`**`auto qos voip trust`**	Identifies this port as connected to a trusted switch or router, and automatically configures QoS for VoIP. Port is configured to trust the CoS label or the DSCP value received on the packet.
`Switch(config-if)#`**`auto qos voip cisco-phone`**	Identifies this port as connected to a Cisco IP Phone, and automatically configures QoS for VoIP.
	NOTE: When using the **auto qos voip cisco-phone** command, if a phone is detected, the port is configured to trust the QoS label received in any packet. If a phone is not detected, the port is set not to trust the QoS label.

Verifying Auto QoS Information: 2960/3560/3750

`Switch#show interface fasthethernet 0/2 switchport`	Displays voice parameters configured on the interface.
`Switch#show auto qos`	Displays the QoS commands entered on all interfaces.
`Switch#show auto qos interface fastethernet 0/11`	Displays the QoS commands entered interface FastEthernet 0/11.

The following commands generate the output shown in Example 8-1:

```
c3750(config)#interface fastethernet 0/2
c3750(config-if)#auto qos voip trust
c3750(config-if)#end
c3750#show running-config
```

Explanations for each of the mapping and queuing commands in Example 8-1 can be found in the IOS Command Reference for each specific switching platform.

Example 8-1   Configuration Generated by the **auto qos** *Command*

```
mls qos map cos-dscp 0 8 16 24 32 46 48 56
!
mls qos srr-queue input bandwidth 90 10
mls qos srr-queue input threshold 1 8 16
mls qos srr-queue input threshold 2 34 66
mls qos srr-queue input buffers 67 33
!
mls qos srr-queue input cos-map queue 1 threshold 2 1
mls qos srr-queue input cos-map queue 1 threshold 3 0
mls qos srr-queue input cos-map queue 2 threshold 1 2
mls qos srr-queue input cos-map queue 2 threshold 2 4 6 7
mls qos srr-queue input cos-map queue 2 threshold 3 3 5
!
mls qos srr-queue input dscp-map queue 1 threshold 2 9 10 11 12 13 14 15
mls qos srr-queue input dscp-map queue 1 threshold 3 0 1 2 3 4 5 6 7
mls qos srr-queue input dscp-map queue 1 threshold 3 32
mls qos srr-queue input dscp-map queue 2 threshold 1 16 17 18 19 20 21 22 23
mls qos srr-queue input dscp-map queue 2 threshold 2 33 34 35 36 37 38 39 48
mls qos srr-queue input dscp-map queue 2 threshold 2 49 50 51 52 53 54 55 56
mls qos srr-queue input dscp-map queue 2 threshold 2 57 58 59 60 61 62 63
mls qos srr-queue input dscp-map queue 2 threshold 3 24 25 26 27 28 29 30 31
mls qos srr-queue input dscp-map queue 2 threshold 3 40 41 42 43 44 45 46 47
!
mls qos srr-queue output cos-map queue 1 threshold 3 5
mls qos srr-queue output cos-map queue 2 threshold 3 3 6 7
mls qos srr-queue output cos-map queue 3 threshold 3 2 4
mls qos srr-queue output cos-map queue 4 threshold 2 1
```

*Example 8-1   Configuration Generated by the **auto qos** Command (Continued)*

```
mls qos srr-queue output cos-map queue 4 threshold 3 0
!
mls qos srr-queue output dscp-map queue 1 threshold 3 40 41 42 43 44 45 46 47
mls qos srr-queue output dscp-map queue 2 threshold 3 24 25 26 27 28 29 30 31
mls qos srr-queue output dscp-map queue 2 threshold 3 48 49 50 51 52 53 54 55
mls qos srr-queue output dscp-map queue 2 threshold 3 56 57 58 59 60 61 62 63
mls qos srr-queue output dscp-map queue 3 threshold 3 16 17 18 19 20 21 22 23
mls qos srr-queue output dscp-map queue 3 threshold 3 32 33 34 35 36 37 38 39
mls qos srr-queue output dscp-map queue 4 threshold 1 8
mls qos srr-queue output dscp-map queue 4 threshold 2 9 10 11 12 13 14 15
mls qos srr-queue output dscp-map queue 4 threshold 3 0 1 2 3 4 5 6 7
!
mls qos queue-set output 1 threshold 1 138 138 92 138
mls qos queue-set output 1 threshold 2 138 138 92 400
mls qos queue-set output 1 threshold 3 36 77 100 318
mls qos queue-set output 1 threshold 4 20 50 67 400
mls qos queue-set output 2 threshold 1 149 149 100 149
mls qos queue-set output 2 threshold 2 118 118 100 235
mls qos queue-set output 2 threshold 3 41 68 100 272
mls qos queue-set output 2 threshold 4 42 72 100 242
!
mls qos queue-set output 1 buffers 10 10 26 54
mls qos queue-set output 2 buffers 16 6 17 61
mls qos
!
interface FastEthernet2/0/2
 no switchport
 ip address 172.19.20.2 255.255.255.0
 srr-queue bandwidth share 10 10 60 20
 priority-queue out
 mls qos trust cos
 auto qos voip trust
!
```

Configuring AutoQoS: 6500

> **TIP:** Although the 6500 series switch is not tested on the SWITCH certification
> exam, these commands have been placed in this command guide because of the
> large number of network professionals working with the 6500 series switch. The
> 6500 series switch uses the Catalyst operating system as opposed to the Cisco IOS
> found on the 2960/3560 series.

`Console> (enable) set qos autoqos`	Applies all global QoS settings to all ports on the switch.
`Console> (enable) set port qos 3/1 - 48 autoqos trust cos`	Applies AutoQoS to ports 3/1–48 and specifies that the ports should trust CoS markings.
`Console> (enable) set port qos 3/1 - 48 autoqos trust dscp`	Applies AutoQoS to ports 3/1–48 and specifies that the ports should trust DSCP markings.
`Console> (enable) set port qos 4/1 autoqos voip ciscoipphone`	Applies AutoQoS settings for any Cisco IP Phone on module 4, port 1.
`Console> (enable) set port qos 4/1 autoqos voip ciscosoftphone`	Applies AutoQoS settings for any Cisco IP SoftPhone on module 4, port 1.

Verifying AutoQoS Information: 6500

`Console> show port qos`	Displays all QoS-related information.
`Console> show port qos 3/1`	Displays all QoS-related information for module 3, port 1.

CHAPTER 9

Integrating Wireless LANs into a Campus Network

This chapter provides information and commands concerning the following topics:

- Wireless roaming and controllers
- The Wireless Services Module (WiSM)
- Configuration example: 4402 WLAN Controller using the Configuration Wizard
- Configuration example: 4402 WLAN Controller using the web interface
- Configuration example: Configuring a 3560 switch to support WLANs and APs
- Configuration example: Configuring a wireless client

Wireless Roaming and Controllers

Layer 2 roaming is moving between access points that reside on a single IP subnet (or VLAN). This is managed by the access points using Inter-Access Point Protocol (IAPP). Roaming between access points that reside in different IP subnets is considered Layer 3 (network layer) roaming. Cisco Mobile IP has been replaced by lightweight access point in combination with Wireless LAN controllers (WLC) for Layer 3 roaming. The WLC handles all the logical functions of the WLAN, including security and QoS. The lightweight access points maintain the functional mechanics of Radio Frequency (RF) data transmission, such as real-time frame exchange and certain real-time portions of MAC management.

WLAN Controllers (WLC) come in the form of appliance controllers such as the 2100, 4400, and 5500 series as well as integrated controllers as modules for ISR routers and 6500 switches. A WLC has also been integrated into a C3750 LAN switch (C3750G).

Data and control messages are encapsulated between the Lightweight Access Point and the WLAN controller using Control And Provisioning of Wireless Access Points (CAPWAP) or Lightweight Access Point Protocol (LWAPP). Control messages are also encrypted.

LAN-deployed Lightweight Access Points (LAP) obtain an IP address via DHCP, and then join a controller via a CAPWAP/LWAPP discovery mechanism.

All client data is switched at the WLAN controller, where VLAN tagging, security measures, and quality of service (QoS) are also applied.

The Remote Edge Access Point (REAP) mode enables a LAP to reside across a wide area network (WAN) link and still be able to communicate with the WLC.

Hybrid REAP (HREAP) are controller-based access points operating in a specific mode. This mode enables customers to configure and control two or three access points in a branch or remote office from the corporate office through a WAN link without the need to deploy a controller in each office but still offer client connectivity if the connection to their controller is lost.

The switch configurations in this chapter support the deployment of a controller-based WLAN solution. The WLC can be a standalone appliance or an integrated module in a C3750, ISR router, or 6500 switch.

Figure 9-1 shows an overview of the switch configuration requirements for the access point and wireless LAN controllers.

Figure 9-1   Switch Configuration Overview in a Controller-Based WLAN Deployment

	Switch Port	QoS	Native VLAN	Management	Data
Standalone AP/Bridge	Trunk	Trust CoS	Management	Native VLAN	Local VLAN
Controller-Based AP	Access	Trust DSCP	AP IP Network	Via Controller	Via Controller
HREAP	Trunk	Trust DSCP	AP IP Network	Via Controller	Local VLAN or via Controller
WLAN Controller	Trunk	Trust CoS	Not Required	Management VLAN	VLAN

Figure 9-2 shows the network diagram to be used as a reference for the switch configurations for standalone APs and HREAPS.

Figure 9-2   Switch Configuration for Standalone APs and HREAPS

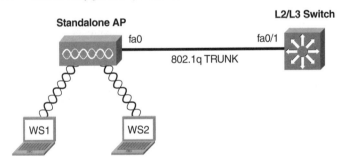

Switch Configuration for Standalone APs and HREAPs

`Switch(config)#`**`interface`** **`fastethernet 0/1`**	Moves to interface configuration mode.
`Switch(config-if)#`**`switchport`** **`encapsulation dot1q`**	Chooses 802.1Q as the trunking protocol.

Switch(config-if)#**switchport trunk native vlan 10**	Defines VLAN 10 at the native VLAN for this trunk.
Switch(config-if)#**switchport allowed vlan 10,20**	Enables traffic for VLAN 10 and 20 on the trunk.
Switch(config-if)#**switchport mode trunk**	Hard codes the port mode to trunk.
Switch(config-if)#**spanning-tree portfast trunk**	Configures the port to start forwarding immediately for every VLAN on the trunk while determining spanning-tree port status.
	NOTE: You can enable this feature when the switch is operating in the per-VLAN spanning-tree plus (PVST+), rapid-PVST+, or multiple spanning-tree (MST) mode. This feature affects all VLANs on the interface. The spanning-tree portfast interface configuration command overrides the global portfast setting.
Switch(config-if)#**mls qos trust cos**	Classifies the inbound packet by Class of Service (CoS) value.
	NOTE: If the packet is untagged, the port default CoS value is used.
Switch(config-if)#**mls qos trust dscp**	Classifies the inbound packet by Differentiated Code Point (DSCP) value.
	NOTE: For a non-IP packet, the packet CoS is used if the packet is tagged. For an untagged packet, the default port CoS value is used.

Switch Configuration for WLC and Controller-Based APs

Figure 9-3 shows the network diagram to be used as a reference for the switch configurations for controller-based APs.

Figure 9-3   Switch Configuration for Controller-Based APs

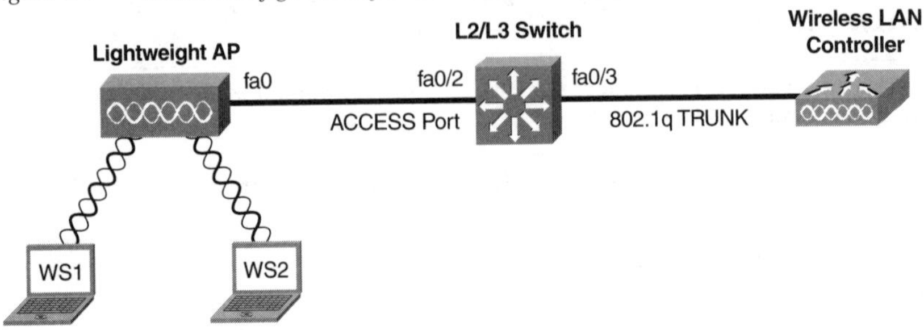

Configuration for the LWAP Connection

Switch(config)#**interface fastethernet 0/2**	Moves to interface configuration mode.
Switch(config-if)#**switchport access vlan 10**	Configures the port to be an access port on VLAN 10.
Switch(config-if)#**switchport mode access**	Hard codes the port to be an access port.
Switch(config-if)#**spanning-tree portfast**	Configures the port to start forwarding immediately while determining spanning-tree status.
Switch(config-if)#**mls qos trust dscp**	Classifies the inbound packet by DSCP value.

Configuration for the WLC Connection

Switch(config)# **interface fastethernet 0/3**	Moves to interface configuration mode.
Switch(config-if)#**switchport trunk encapsulation dot1q**	Chooses 802.1Q as the trunking protocol.
Switch(config-if)#**switchport trunk native vlan 99**	Defines VLAN 99 at the native VLAN for this trunk.
Switch(config-if)#**switchport trunk allowed vlan 10,20**	Enables traffic for VLAN 10 and 20 on the trunk.
Switch(config-if)#**switchport mode trunk**	Hard codes the port as a trunk.

Switch(config-if)#**spanning-tree portfast trunk**	Configures the port to start forwarding immediately for every VLAN on the trunk while determining spanning-tree port status.
Switch(config-if)#**mls qos trust cos**	Classifies the inbound packet by CoS value.

Switch Configuration for 4400 Series Controllers (EtherChannel)

Figure 9-4 shows the network diagram to be used as a reference for the switch configurations for 4400 series controller using an EtherChannel.

Figure 9-4   Switch Configuration for 4400 Controller with EtherChannel

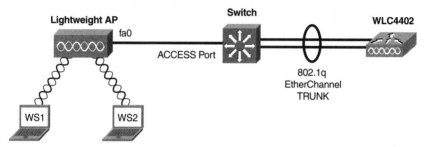

Switch(config)#**interface gigabitethernet 0/1**	Moves to interface configuration mode.
Switch(config-if)#**channel-group 1 mode on**	Assigns the gigabit Ethernet port 0/1 to EtherChannel group 1.
Switch(config)#**interface gigabitethernet 0/2**	Moves to interface configuration mode for gigabitethernet 0/2.
Switch(config-if)#**channel-group 1 mode on**	Assigns the gigabit Ethernet port 0/2 to EtherChannel group 1.
Switch(config)#**interface port-channel 1**	Creates the port-channel logical interface port-channel 1.
Switch(config-if)#**switchport trunk encapsulation dot1q**	Chooses 802.1Q as the trunking protocol for the port channel.
Switch(config-if)#**switchport trunk native vlan 99**	Defines VLAN 99 at the native VLAN for this trunk.

`Switch(config-if)#switchport trunk allowed vlan 10,20`	Enables traffic for VLAN 10 and 20 on the trunk.
`Switch(config-if)#switchport mode trunk`	Hard codes the port as a trunk.
`Switch(config-if)#spanning-tree portfast trunk`	Configures the port to start forwarding immediately for every VLAN on the trunk while determining spanning-tree port status.
`Switch(config-if)#mls qos trust cos`	Classifies the inbound packet by CoS value.

The Wireless Services Module

The Cisco Wireless Services Module (WiSM) is a member of the Cisco wireless LAN controller family. It works in conjunction with Cisco Aironet Lightweight Access Points (LAP), the Cisco Wireless Control System (WCS), and the Cisco wireless location appliance to deliver a secure and unified wireless solution that supports wireless data, voice, and video applications.

The Cisco WiSM consists of two separate Cisco 4404 controllers on a single module. The first controller is considered the WiSM-A card, and the second controller is considered the WiSM-B card. Interfaces and IP addressing must be considered on both cards independently.

There are three main interfaces on each controller of the WiSM in which it communicates:

- Management interface is the default interface for in-band management of the controller and connectivity to enterprise services such as AAA server.
- AP-Manager interface is used as the source IP address for all Layer 3 communications between the controller and the lightweight access points.
- Service-port interface is local to the switch chassis and is used for communication between Cisco WiSM and Catalyst Supervisor 720 over a Gigabit interface on the Supervisor and Service-Port in the Cisco WiSM.

Configuring Communication Between the Supervisor 720 and Cisco WiSM

Figure 9-5 shows the network diagram to be used as a reference for the 6500 switch configurations for the WiSM's controllers.

Figure 9-5   6500 Switch with WiSM Topology

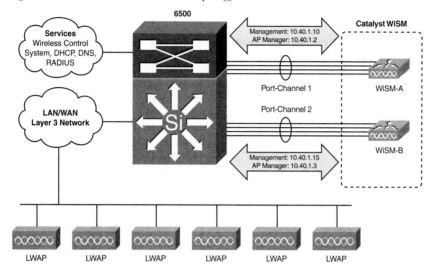

Step 1. Create a VLAN local to the Sup720 chassis, which is used for communication between Cisco WiSM controllers and Catalyst Supervisor 720 over a Gigabit interface on the Supervisor and Service-Port in the Cisco WiSM.

`Sup720(config)#`**`vlan 222`**	Creates VLAN 222 for the Service-Port IP segment.
`Sup720(config)#`**`interface vlan 222`**	Moves to SVI configuration mode.
`Sup720(config-if)#`**`ip address`** **`192.168.222.1 255.255.255.0`**	Assigns an IP address for the Service-Port segment.
`Sup720(config-if)#`**`no shutdown`**	Turns on the interface.
`Sup720(config-if)#`**`exit`**	Returns to global configuration mode.

Step 2. Create a DHCP scope for the service port of the Cisco WiSM in Supervisor 720 or on a standalone DHCP server. Then associate the previous VLAN for the service port.

`Sup720(config)#`**`ip dhcp pool WISM-`** **`SERVICE-PORT`**	Moves to DHCP configuration mode for pool WISM-SERVICE-PORT.

`Sup720(dhcp-config)#`**`network`** **`192.168.222.0 255.255.255.0`**	Configures the IP segment used for Service-Port addressing.
`Sup720(dhcp-config)#`**`default-router`** **`192.168.222.1`**	Configures the gateway IP for the Service-Port IP segment.
	NOTE: Each WiSM controller provides through DHCP an address from the 192.168.222.0/24 segment. This is the initial communication conduit between the switch's supervisor engine and each of the WiSM controllers.

Step 3.   Configure VLAN 222 to communicate with the Service-Port.

`Sup720(config)#`**`wism service-vlan 222`**	Links a common IP segment between the Sup720 and the WiSM controllers.
	NOTE: The Service-Port on each of the two controllers requests an IP address from the Sup720 from the 192.168.222.0/24 segment.
	NOTE: The **show wism status** command displays the IP addresses that were assigned to each controller's Service-Port Interfaces.

Step 4.   Create the VLAN in the Supervisor 720 that communicates with the management and AP-manager ports of the Cisco WiSM controller.

`Sup720(config)#`**`vlan 40`**	Creates VLAN 40 for the Management and AP-Manager IP segment.
`Sup720(config)#`**`interface vlan 40`**	Moves to SVI configuration mode.
`Sup720(config-if)#`**`ip address`** **`10.40.1.1 255.255.0.0`**	Assigns an IP address for the Management/AP Manager segment.
`Sup720(config-if)#`**`no shutdown`**	Turns on the interface.
`Sup720(config-if)#`**`exit`**	Moves to global configuration mode.

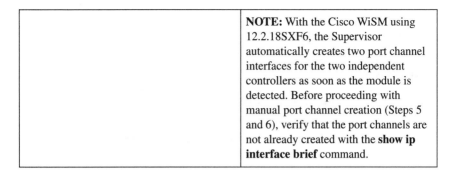

	NOTE: With the Cisco WiSM using 12.2.18SXF6, the Supervisor automatically creates two port channel interfaces for the two independent controllers as soon as the module is detected. Before proceeding with manual port channel creation (Steps 5 and 6), verify that the port channels are not already created with the **show ip interface brief** command.

Step 5.   Create two port-channel interfaces for the two independent controllers in the Cisco WiSM, and assign VLAN 40 as the native interface.

`Sup720(config)#`**`interface port-channel 1`**	Creates a logical interface Port-Channel 1 for the EtherChannel to controller 1 in the WiSM.
`Sup720(config-if)#`**`switchport`**	Configures the port to be a Layer 2 switched port.
`Sup720(config-if)#`**`switchport trunk encapsulation dot1q`**	Chooses 802.1Q as the trunking protocol for the port channel.
`Sup720(config-if)#`**`switchport trunk native vlan 40`**	Defines VLAN 40 at the native VLAN for this trunk.
`Sup720(config-if)#`**`switchport mode trunk`**	Hard codes the port as a trunk.
`Sup720(config-if)#`**`mls qos trust dscp`**	Classifies the inbound packet by DSCP value.
`Sup720(config-if)#`**`spanning-tree portfast`**	Configures the port to start forwarding immediately for every VLAN on the trunk while determining spanning-tree port status.
`Sup720(config)#`**`interface port-channel 2`**	Creates a logical interface Port-Channel for the EtherChannel to controller 2 in the WiSM.
`Sup720(config-if)#`**`switchport`**	Configures the port to be a Layer 2 switched port.

`Sup720(config-if)#`**`switchport trunk`** **`encapsulation dot1q`**	Chooses 802.1Q as the trunking protocol for the port channel.
`Sup720(config-if)#`**`switchport trunk`** **`native vlan 40`**	Defines VLAN 40 at the native VLAN for this trunk.
`Sup720(config-if)#`**`switchport mode`** **`trunk`**	Hard codes the port as a trunk.
`Sup720(config-if)#`**`mls qos trust dscp`**	Classifies the inbound packet by DSCP value.
`Sup720(config-if)#`**`spanning-tree`** **`portfast`**	Configures the port to start forwarding immediately for every VLAN on the trunk while determining spanning-tree port status.

Step 6. Configure the Gigabit Ethernet interfaces as trunk ports with VLAN 40 as the native VLAN.

`Sup720(config)#`**`interface range`** **`gigabitethernet3/1 - 4`**	Moves to interface range configuration mode.
	NOTE: The Gigabit interfaces 3/1–4 correspond to the first controller in Cisco WiSM and should be a member of channel group one.
`Sup720(config-if)#`**`switchport`**	Configures the ports to be a Layer 2 switched port.
`Sup720(config-if)#`**`switchport trunk`** **`encapsulation dot1q`**	Chooses 802.1Q as the trunking protocol for the port channel.
`Sup720(config-if)#`**`switchport mode`** **`trunk`**	Hard codes the port as a trunk.
`Sup720(config-if)#`**`switchport trunk`** **`native vlan 40`**	Defines VLAN 40 at the native VLAN for this trunk.
`Sup720(config-if)#`**`spanning-tree`** **`portfast`**	Configures the port to start forwarding immediately for every VLAN on the trunk while determining spanning-tree port status.
`Sup720(config-if)#`**`channel-group 1`** **`mode on`**	Creates channel group 1 and assigns interfaces 3/1–4 as part of it.

Sup720(config-if)#**no shutdown**	Turns on the interfaces.
Sup720(config-if)#**exit**	Returns to global configuration mode.
Sup720(config)#**interface range gigabitethernet3/5 - 8**	Moves to interface range configuration mode.
	NOTE: The Gigabit interfaces 3/5–8 correspond to the second controller in Cisco WiSM and should be a member of channel group two.
Sup720(config-if)#**switchport**	Configures the ports to be a Layer 2 switched port.
Sup720(config-if)#**switchport trunk encapsulation dot1q**	Chooses 802.1Q as the trunking protocol for the port channel.
Sup720(config-if)#**switchport mode trunk**	Hard codes the port as a trunk.
Sup720(config-if)#**switchport trunk native vlan 40**	Defines VLAN 40 at the native VLAN for this trunk.
Sup720(config-if)#**spanning-tree portfast**	Configures the port to start forwarding immediately for every VLAN on the trunk while determining spanning-tree port status.
Sup720(config-if)#**channel-group 2 mode on**	Creates channel group 1 and assigns interfaces 3/5–8 as part of it.
Sup720(config-if)#**no shutdown**	Turns on the interfaces.
Sup720(config-if)#**exit**	Returns to global configuration mode.

Step 7.   The following commands can be used to configure the port-channel with native and allowed VLANs. In this case, VLAN 40 is configured as the native VLAN.

Sup720(config)#**wism module 3 controller 1 native-vlan 40**	Configures VLAN 40 as the native VLAN on the EtherChannel trunk between the Sup720 and controller 1 of the WiSM module in slot 3.

`Sup720(config)#`**`wism module 3`** **`controller 2 native-vlan 40`**	Configures VLAN 40 as the native VLAN on the EtherChannel trunk between the Sup720 and controller 2 of the WiSM module in slot 3.
`Sup720(config)#`**`wism module 3`** **`controller 1 allowed-vlan 30,40`**	Enables VLAN 30 and 40 on the EtherChannel trunk between the Sup720 and controller 1 of the WiSM module in slot 3.
`Sup720(config)#`**`wism module 3`** **`controller 2 allowed-vlan 30,40`**	Enables VLAN 30 and 40 on the EtherChannel trunk between the Sup720 and controller 2 of the WiSM module in slot 3.
`Sup720(config)#`**`wism module 3`** **`controller 1 qos trust cos`**	Classifies the frame inbound to the WiSM controller 1 by CoS value.
`Sup720(config)#`**`wism module 3`** **`controller 2 qos trust cos`**	Classifies the frame inbound to the WiSM controller 2 by CoS value.
	NOTE: The controllers in the Cisco WiSM are automatically assigned to a channel group, usually a high number, and the necessary commands are added automatically.

The Initial WiSM Configuration

The initial preparation of the switch for the WiSM is now complete. To start the WiSM configuration, initiate a session to the WiSM from the supervisor.

`Sup720#`**`session 3 processor 1`**	Initiates a session to controller 1 of the WiSM in slot 3.

After the administrator establishes a session with the Cisco WiSM, the basic configuration is completed with the help of the setup script. An example of this script is shown in the following configuration example. With the completion of basic configuration, the administrator can configure the Cisco WiSM controller through the console CLI or through the Cisco WiSM controller web interface. An administrator needs to configure WiSM-A and WiSM-B separately in the Cisco WiSM module, initially from the CLI and then from the web interface.

Configuration Example: 4402 WLAN Controller Using the Configuration Wizard

NOTE: In the WLC Configuration Wizard, all available options appear in brackets after each parameter. The default value appears in all uppercase letters.

Commands are case sensitive.

```
    .o88b. d888888b .d8888.  .o88b.  .d88b.
   d8P  Y8   '88'   88'  YP d8P  Y8 .8P  Y8.
   8P         88    '8bo.  8P        88    88
   8b         88     'Y8b. 8b        88    88
   Y8b  d8  .88.   db   8D Y8b  d8 '8b  d8'
    'Y88P' Y888888P '8888Y'  'Y88P'  'Y88P'
   Model AIR-WLC4402-12-K9   S/N: XXXXXXXXXXX
Net:
 PHY DEVICE  : Found Intel LXT971A PHY at 0x01
FEC ETHERNET
IDE:   Bus 0: OK
 Device 0: Model: STI Flash 7.4.0 Firm: 01.25.06
   Ser#: XXXXXXXXXX
           Type: Removable Hard Disk
           Capacity: 245.0 MB = 0.2 GB (501760
           x 512)
 Device 1: not available
```

`Booting Primary Image...`
 	
`Press <ESC> now for additional boot options...`
 	
`***** External Console Active *****`
 	
`     Boot Options`
 	
`Please choose an option from below:`
 	
`1. Run primary image (version 4.0.179.8) (active)`
 	
`2. Run backup image (version 4.0.179.8)`
 	
`3. Manually update images`
 	
`4. Change active boot image`
 	
`5. Clear Configuration`
 	
`Please enter your choice: 1`
 	
`Detecting Hardware . . .`
	Select **1** to continue to boot the primary image—this is the default choice.
	
	Select **2** to boot the backup image (the image used before the last software upgrade).
	
	Select **3** for manual upgrade of image files.
	
	Select **4** to set the backup image as the primary image.
	
	Select **5** to set the configuration back to the factory default and start the CLI Setup Wizard using the current software.

	NOTE: Option 3 is for recovery only. Do not select this option unless you have the required files and are instructed to do so by the Cisco Technical Assistance Center (TAC).
`<OUTPUT CUT>`	
`Welcome to the Cisco Wizard Configuration Tool` `Use the '-' character to backup`	Press the hyphen key if you need to return to the previous command line.

`System Name [Cisco_xx:xx:xx]:`	Enters the system name for the controller. Length is up to 32 ASCII characters. If no name is entered, a default of Cisco Controller is used.
`Enter Administrative User Name (24 characters max):` **cisco** `Enter Administrative Password (24 characters max):` **password**	Assigns the administrative username and password. The default username and password are admin and admin.
`Service Interface IP Address Configuration [none][DHCP]:`**DHCP**	Enter **DHCP** if you want the controller's Service-Port interface to obtain its IP address from a DHCP server. Enter **none** if you want to set one statically or if you don't want to use the service port.
	NOTE: The Service-Port interface controls communications through the service port. Its IP address must be on a different subnet from the management and AP-manager interfaces. This enables you to manage the controller directly or through a dedicated management network to ensure service access during network downtime.

	NOTE: If you do not want to use the service port, enter **0.0.0.0** for the IP address and subnet mask. If you want to statically assign an address and mask, do so on the next two lines when prompted.
`Enable Link Aggregation (LAG) [yes][NO]:`	Enables link aggregation, if desired.
`Management Interface IP Address: `**`172.16.1.100`** `Management Interface Netmask: `**`255.255.255.0`** `Management Interface Default Router: `**`172.16.1.1`** `Management Interface VLAN Identifier (0 = untagged): `**`0`** `Management Interface Port Num [1 to 2]: `**`1`** `Management Interface DHCP Server IP Address: `**`172.16.1.1`**	Assigns IP address, netmask, default router IP address, optional VLAN identifier of the management interface, and port number of the management interface. Assigns the IP address of the DHCP server that will assign addresses to the management interface and Service-Port interface.
	NOTE: The VLAN identifier should be set to match the switch interface configuration.
	NOTE: The management interface is the default interface for in-band management of the controller and connectivity to enterprise services such as an authentication, authorization, and accounting (AAA) server.
`AP Transport Mode [layer2][LAYER3]:`	Sets the AP transport layer.

`AP Manager Interface IP Address:` **`172.16.100.100`**
 	
`AP Manager Interface Netmask:` **`255.255.255.0`**
 	
`AP Manager Interface Default Router:`
`172.16.100.1`
 	
`AP Manager Interface VLAN Identifier (0 =`
`untagged):` **`100`**
 	
`AP Manager Interface Port Num [1 to 2]:` **`1`**
 	
`AP Manager Interface DHCP Server (172.16.1.1):`
`172.16.100.1`
	Assigns the IP address, netmask, default router IP address, optional VLAN identifier, and port number of the AP manager interface.
	
	Assigns the IP address of the DHCP server that will assign addresses to the APs.

	NOTE: The AP manager interface is used for Layer 3 communication between the controller and the LAPs. It must have a unique IP address and is usually configured as the same VLAN or IP subnet as the management interface, but is not required to be.
	NOTE: If the AP manager interface is on the same subnet as the management interface, the same DHCP server is used for the AP manager interface and the management interface.
`Virtual Gateway IP Address:` **`1.1.1.1`**	Assigns an IP address to the controller's virtual interface.
	NOTE: Because the virtual gateway will not be routed, use a fictitious, unassigned IP address, such as 1.1.1.1. All controllers within a mobility group must be configured with the same virtual interface IP address.

`Mobility/RF Group Name:` **`SWITCH`**	Assigns the name of the mobility group/RF group to which this controller belongs.
`Network Name (SSID):` **`SWITCH`**	Assigns the service set identifier (SSID).
`Allow Static IP Addresses [YES][no]:`	Enter **yes** (or press the Enter key) if you want to allow clients to assign their own IP addresses. Enter **no** if you want to force clients to use IP addresses from a DHCP server.

`Configure a RADIUS Server now? [YES][no]:` **`no`**
 `Warning! The default WLAN security policy`
 `requires a RADIUS server.`
 `Please see documentation for more details.`
	Enter **yes** if you want to configure a RADIUS server now. Enter **no** if you do not want to do so at this time.

`Enter Country Code (enter 'help' for a list of countries) [US]:` **`US`**	Assigns the country code.

`Enable 802.11b Network [YES][no]:`
 `Enable 802.11a Network [YES][no]:`
 `Enable 802.11g Network [YES][no]:`
	Enter **yes** (or press the Enter key) to enable each of the 802.11b, a, or g LAP networks. Enter **no** to disable.

`Enable Auto-RF [YES][no]:`	Enter **yes** to enable or **no** to disable the Radio Resource Management (RRM) auto-RF feature.
	NOTE: The auto-RF feature enables the controller to automatically form an RF group with other controllers.
`Configuration saved!` `Resetting system with new configuration...`	Saves configuration, and then automatically reboots the controller.

	NOTE: This is the end of the wizard. From here on are examples of commands used to continue with the configuration and verification of the controller.
`<Output Cut>`	

`(Cisco Controller)`
 	
`Enter User Name (or 'Recover-Config' this one-time only to reset configuration to factory defaults)`
 	
`User: `**`cisco`**
 	
`Password:********`
	Enter your username and password to log in to the controller.

`(Cisco Controller) >`**`config prompt`** **`WLAN_Controller`**	Changes the controller prompt to WLAN_Controller. The length of this prompt is 31 alphanumeric characters.
`(WLAN_Controller) >`**`config network telnet enable`**	Enables Telnet access to the WLAN controller. By default, controllers block Telnet connections.
`(WLAN_Controller) >`**`config network webmode enable`**	Enables HTTP access to the WLAN controller.
	NOTE: HTTPS access is enabled by default; unsecured HTTP is not.
`(WLAN_Controller) >`**`config serial timeout 3`**	Sets automatic logout of the CLI to 3 minutes.

	NOTE: The default timeout for the CLI is 0 minutes. The range of the **config serial timeout** command is 0 to 160, measured in minutes, where 0 represents never logging out.
(WLAN_Controller) >**save config** Are you sure you want to save? (y/n) **y** Configuration Saved!	Saves the configuration.
(WLAN_Controller) >**show interface summary**	Displays the current interface configuration.
(WLAN_Controller) >**show run-config**	Displays the current configuration.
(WLAN_Controller) >**show ap summary**	Displays a summary of all Cisco 1000 series LAPs attached to the controller.
(WLAN_Controller) >**show wlan summary**	Displays a summary of the WLANs.
(WLAN_Controller) > **show port summary**	Displays the status of the controller's distribution system ports.

After configuration is complete, you can open up a web browser and connect to the device. Figure 9-6 shows the GUI login screen. Using the preceding configuration as a guide, connect to 172.16.1.100. If you are connecting to an unconfigured controller, use the address 192.168.1.1.

Figure 9-6   GUI Login Screen

Figure 9-7 shows the login screen after the Login button has been pressed.

Figure 9-7   GUI Login Screen After the Login Button Has Been Pressed

Figure 9-8 shows the main page after a successful login.

Figure 9-8   Main Page

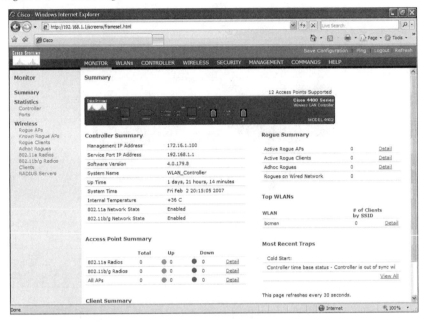

Configuration Example: 4402 WLAN Controller Using the Web Interface

NOTE: The Cisco 4400 series WLAN controller supports the initial configuration via a web browser through the service port. The default address of the unconfigured controller is 192.168.1.1. The default username and password are both admin.

NOTE: Cisco recommends using Internet Explorer 6.0 with Service Pack 1 (SP1) or later with full switch web interface functionality.

There are known issues with Opera, Mozilla, and Netscape.

Refer to Figure 9-6 and Figure 9-7 for the GUI login screen. If you use the default address of 192.168.1.1 and the default username/password combination of admin/admin, the GUI Configuration Wizard appears. Figure 9-9 shows the first screen of the GUI Configuration Wizard.

Figure 9-9   First Screen of the GUI Configuration Wizard

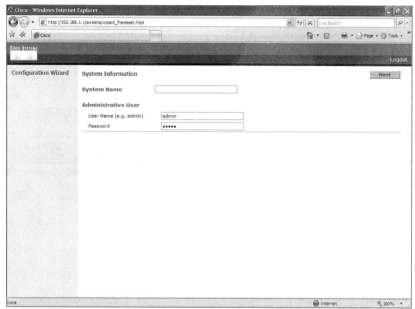

Figure 9-10 shows the second screen of the GUI Configuration Wizard. This is where you configure the IP address and netmask of the service interface and enable DHCP, if desired.

Figure 9-10   Service Interface Configuration of the GUI Configuration Wizard

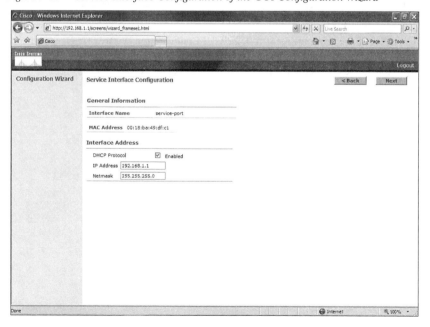

Figure 9-11 shows the third screen of the GUI Configuration Wizard. This is where you assign the IP address, netmask, default router IP address, optional VLAN identifier of the management interface, and port number of the management interface. You also configure the IP address of the DHCP server that assigns addresses to the APs. Note that if you leave the VLAN identifier as zero, it means the interface is untagged.

Figure 9-11   Management Interface Configuration Screen of the GUI Configuration Wizard

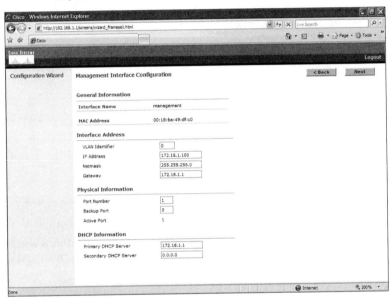

Figure 9-12 shows the fourth screen of the GUI Configuration Wizard. This is where you set the AP transport layer mode along with the RF mobility domain name and the country code. Note that the screen scrolls down to list more country codes.

Figure 9-12   Miscellaneous Configuration of the GUI Configuration Wizard

Figure 9-13 shows the fifth screen of the GUI Configuration Wizard. This is where you assign the IP address, netmask, default router IP address, optional VLAN identifier, and port number of the AP manager interface. You also assign the address of the DHCP server. If the AP manager interface is on the same subnet as the management interface, the same DHCP server is used for the AP manager interface and the management interface.

Figure 9-13   AP Manager Interface Configuration Screen of the GUI Configuration Wizard

Figure 9-14 shows the sixth screen of the GUI Configuration Wizard. This is where you assign the IP address of the virtual interface. Because the virtual gateway will not be routed, use a fictitious, unassigned IP address, such as 1.1.1.1. All controllers within a mobility group must be configured with the same virtual interface IP address.

Figure 9-14   Virtual Interface Configuration Screen of the GUI Configuration Wizard

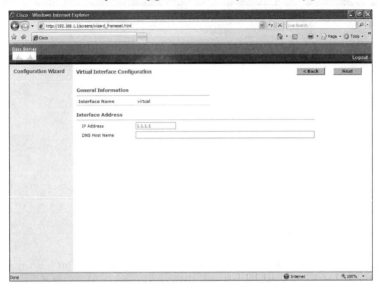

Figure 9-15 shows the seventh screen of the GUI Configuration Wizard. This is where you configure the WLAN SSID, along with general policies and security policies. You also set the 802.1x parameters here.

Figure 9-15   WLAN Policy Configuration Screen of the GUI Configuration Wizard

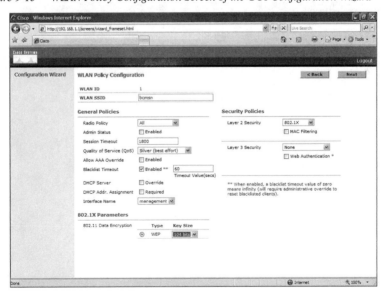

Figure 9-16 shows the eighth screen of the GUI Configuration Wizard. This is where you configure your RADIUS server. In this example, no RADIUS server was wanted, so this screen was left to the default settings.

Figure 9-16   RADIUS Server Configuration Screen of the GUI Configuration Wizard

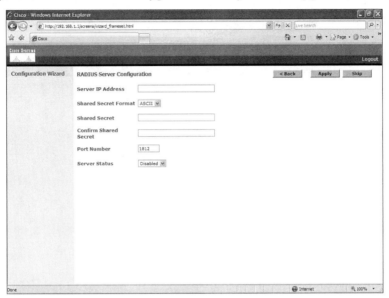

Figure 9-17 shows the ninth screen of the GUI Configuration Wizard. This is where you enable the network status of your wireless technologies—802.11a/b/g and Auto-RF.

Figure 9-17   802.11 Configuration Screen of the GUI Configuration Wizard

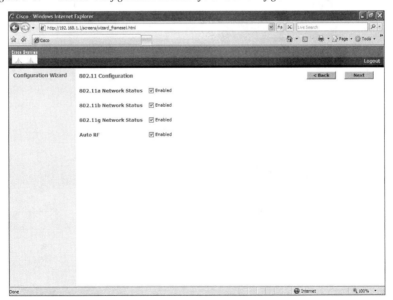

Figure 9-18 shows the tenth screen of the GUI Configuration Wizard. At this point, the configuration is complete. The pop-up appears after you click the Save and Reboot button. The configuration saves, and the controller then restarts.

Figure 9-18   Configuration Wizard Complete Screen of the GUI Configuration Wizard

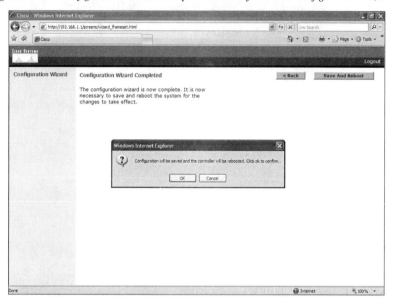

After the system has been rebooted, HTTP will no longer work. You must use HTTPS. Figure 9-19 shows the login screen in HTTPS.

Figure 9-19   Login Screen in HTTPS

To enable HTTP access, choose the Management tab on the top of the page, and then select HTTP on the left side of the screen, as illustrated in Figure 9-20. Choose the Enabled option for HTTP Access. Note that in Figure 9-20, HTTP has not been enabled yet but HTTPS has.

Figure 9-20   Enabling HTTP Access

To change the controller name, choose the Management tab on the top of the page, and then select SNMP on the left side of the screen, as illustrated in Figure 9-21. Here you can change the controller name, add a description of the location of the controller, and add the contact information of the controller administrator.

Figure 9-21   Changing Controller Name

Figure 9-22 shows a summary of the menu bar in the GUI of the WLC.

Figure 9-22   WLC Web Menu Bar

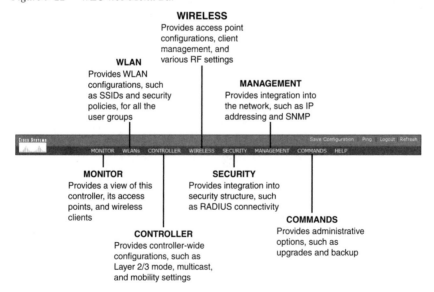

Configuration Example: Configuring a 3560 Switch to Support WLANs and APs

Figure 9-23 shows the network topology for the configuration that follows, which shows how to configure a 3560 switch to support WLANs and APs.

Figure 9-23   Topology for WLAN/AP Support Configuration on a 3560 Switch

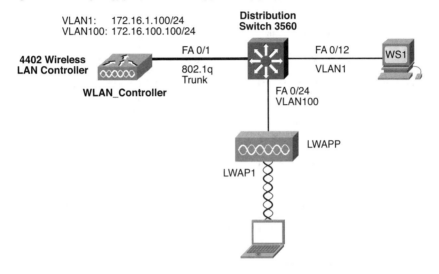

Switch>**enable**	Moves to privileged mode.
Switch#**configure terminal**	Moves to global configuration mode.
Switch(config)#**hostname 3560**	Sets the host name of the switch.
3560(config)#**vlan 1**	Enters VLAN-configuration mode.
3560(config-vlan)#**name Management**	Assigns a name to VLAN 1.
3560(config-vlan)#**exit**	Returns to global configuration mode.
3560(config)#**vlan 100**	Creates VLAN 100 and enters VLAN-configuration mode.
3560(config-vlan)#**name Wireless**	Assigns a name to VLAN 100.
3560(config-vlan)#**exit**	Returns to global configuration mode.
3560(config)#**interface vlan 1**	Moves to interface configuration mode.

`3560(config-if)#`**`ip address 172.16.1.1 255.255.255.0`**	Assigns IP address and netmask.
`3560(config-if)#`**`no shutdown`**	Enables the interface.
`3560(config-if)#`**`interface vlan 100`**	Moves to interface configuration mode.
`3560(config-if)#`**`ip address 172.16.100.1 255.255.255.0`**	Assigns IP address and netmask.
`3560(config-if)#`**`no shutdown`**	Enables the interface.
`3560(config-if)#`**`exit`**	Returns to global configuration mode.
`3560(config)#`**`ip dhcp pool wireless`**	Creates a DHCP pool called wireless and enters DHCP configuration mode.
`3560(config-dhcp)#`**`network 172.16.100.0 255.255.255.0`**	Defines the range of addresses to be leased.
`3560(config-dhcp)#`**`default router 172.16.100.1`**	Defines the address of the default router for the client.
`3560(config-dhcp)#`**`exit`**	Returns to global configuration mode.
`3560(config)#`**`interface fastethernet 0/1`**	Moves to interface configuration mode.
`3560(config-if)#`**`description link to WLAN_Controller`**	Creates locally significant description.
`3560(config-if)#`**`switchport mode trunk`**	Makes this interface a trunk port.
`3560(config-if)#`**`interface fastethernet 0/24`**	Moves to interface configuration mode for interface fastethernet 0/24.
`3560(config-if)#`**`description link to Access Point`**	Creates locally significant description.
`3560(config-if)#`**`switchport mode access`**	Makes this interface an access port.
`3560(config-if)#`**`switchport access vlan 100`**	Assigns this interface to VLAN 100.
`3560(config-if)#`**`spanning-tree portfast`**	Enables PortFast on this interface.
`3560(config-if)#`**`exit`**	Returns to global configuration mode.
`3560(config)#`**`exit`**	Returns to privileged mode.
`3560#`**`copy running-config startup-config`**	Saves the configuration to NVRAM.

Configuration Example: Configuring a Wireless Client

Refer to Figure 9-23, which shows the network topology for the following configuration on how to configure a Cisco Aironet wireless client adapter:

Step 1.   Install a Cisco Aironet Wireless Adapter into an open slot on your laptop.

Step 2.   Load the Cisco Aironet Desktop Utility software onto your laptop.

Step 3.   If necessary, reboot your machine, and then run the Aironet Desktop Utility program.

Step 4.   Open the Profiles Management tab and click New (see Figure 9-24).

Figure 9-24   Profile Management Screen

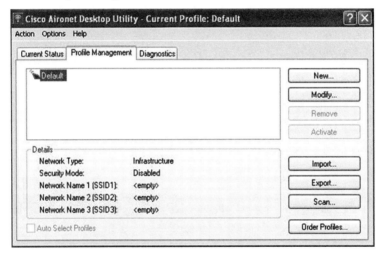

Step 5.   Enter your profile name, client name, and SSID (see Figure 9-25).

Figure 9-25   SSID Configuration

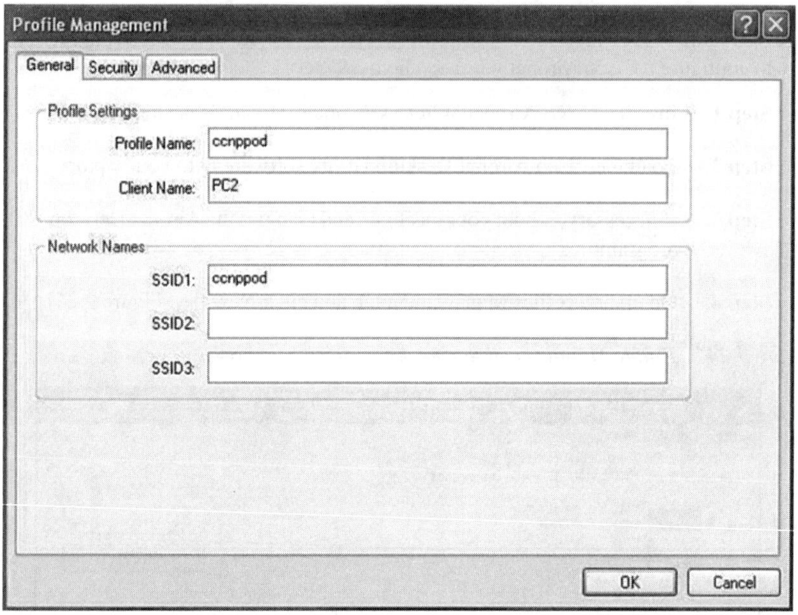

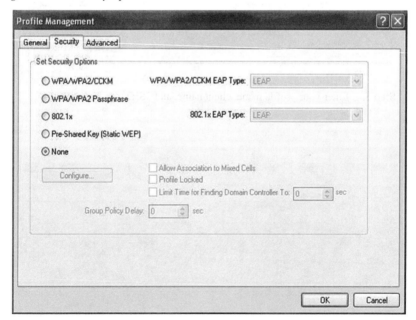

Step 6.   Open the Security tab and choose None (see Figure 9-26).

Figure 9-26   Security Options

Step 7.   Open the Advanced tab. Uncheck the 5GHz 54 Mbps, because you are not using 802.11a. Then click OK (see Figure 9-27).

Figure 9-27   Advanced Options

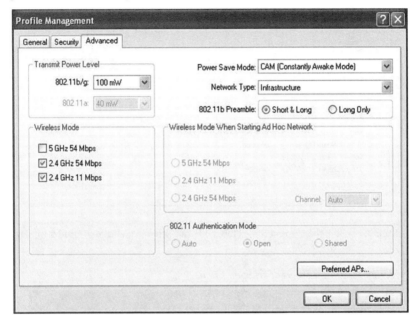

Step 8.   After clicking OK, you are returned to the Profile Management screen. In addition to the default profile, there is a new profile called *ccnppod*. Select the *ccnppod* profile and click the Activate button. After clicking the Activate button, the screen looks like Figure 9-28.

Figure 9-28   ccnppod Profile Activated

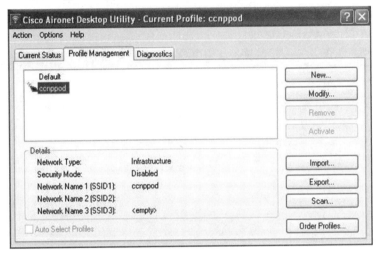

Step 9.   Click the Current Status tab, and your screen should look similar to Figure 9-29.

Figure 9-29   Current Status of ccnppod Profile

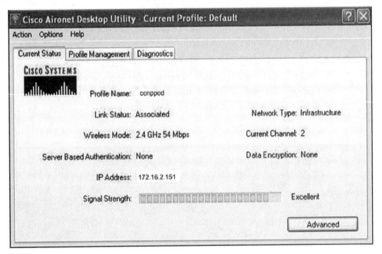

Private VLAN Catalyst Switch Support Matrix

Private VLANs (PVLAN) provide Layer (L2) isolation between ports within the same VLAN. Table A-1 summarizes the support of the PVLAN feature in Cisco Catalyst switches.

Table A-1   Catalyst Switch PVLAN Support Matrix

Catalyst Platform	PVLAN Supported Minimum Software Version	Isolated VLAN	PVLAN Edge (Protected Port)	Community VLAN
Catalyst 6500/6000— Hybrid mode (CatOS on Supervisor and Cisco IOS on MSFC)	5.4(1) on Supervisor and 12.0(7)XE1 on MSFC	Yes	Not Supported	Yes
Catalyst 6500/6000— Native mode (Cisco IOS System software on both Supervisor and MSFC)	12.1(8a)EX, 12.1(11b)E1, and later	Yes	Not Supported	Yes
Catalyst 5500/5000	Not Supported	Not Supported	Not Supported	Not Supported
Catalyst 4500/4000— CatOS	6.2(1)	Yes	Not Supported	Yes
Catalyst 4500/4000— Cisco IOS	12.1(8a)EW	Yes	Not Supported	Yes. 12.2(20)EW onward.
Catalyst 3550	Not Supported	Not Supported	Yes. 12.1(4)EA1 onward.	Not Supported
Catalyst 2950	Not Supported	Not Supported	Yes. 12.0(5.2)WC1, 12.1(4)EA1, and later.	Not Supported
Catalyst 2900XL/ 3500XL	Not Supported	Not Supported	Yes. 12.0(5)XU (on 8MB switches only) onward.	Not Supported

Table A-1   Catalyst Switch PVLAN Support Matrix (Continued)

Catalyst Platform	PVLAN Supported Minimum Software Version	Isolated VLAN	PVLAN Edge (Protected Port)	Community VLAN
Catalyst 2948G-L3/ 4908G-L3	Not Supported	Not Supported	Not Supported	Not Supported
Catalyst 1900	Not Supported	Not Supported	Not Supported	Not Supported
Catalyst 8500	Not Supported	Not Supported	Not Supported	Not Supported
Catalyst 3560	12.2(20)SE—EMI	Yes	Yes. 12.1(19)EA1 onward.	Yes
Catalyst 3750	12.2(20)SE—EMI	Yes	Yes. 12.1(11)AX onward.	Yes
Catalyst 3750 Metro	12.2(25)EY—EMI	Yes	Yes. 12.1(14)AX onward.	Yes
Catalyst 2940	Not Supported	Not Supported	Yes. 12.1(13)AY onward.	Not Supported
Catalyst 2948G/2980G	6.2	Yes	Not Supported	Yes
Catalyst 2955	Not Supported	Not Supported	Yes. 12.1(6)EA2 onward.	Not Supported
Catalyst 2970	Not Supported	Not Supported	Yes. 12.1(11)AX onward.	Not Supported
Catalyst 2960	Not Supported	Not Supported	Yes. 12.2(25)FX and later.	Not Supported
Catalyst Express 500	Not Supported	Not Supported	Not Supported	Not Supported

Create Your Own Journal Here

Even though I have tried to be as complete as possible in this reference guide, invariably I will have left something out that you need in your specific day-to-day activities. That is why this section is here. Use these blank lines to enter in your own notes, making this reference guide your own personalized journal.

GO FURTHER, FASTER.
BECOME CERTIFIED.

Stop thinking about your potential. Realize it. Take your training, skills and knowledge to the next level. Get Cisco Certified through Pearson VUE.

Take your Cisco Career Certification exam at one of more than 4,400 conveniently located Pearson VUE® Authorized Test Centers worldwide to experience a no-hassle test experience. To register at a test center near you, simply visit PearsonVUE.com/Cisco.

PEARSON VUE

CCNP SWITCH
Portable Command Guide

All the SWITCH 642-813 Commands
in One Compact, Portable Resource

ciscopress.com

Scott Empson
Hans Roth

FREE Online Edition

Your purchase of **CCNP SWITCH Portable Command Guide** includes access to a free online edition for 45 days through the Safari Books Online subscription service. Nearly every Cisco Press book is available online through Safari Books Online, along with more than 5,000 other technical books and videos from publishers such as Addison-Wesley Professional, Que, Exam Cram, IBM Press, O'Reilly, Prentice Hall, and Sams.

SAFARI BOOKS ONLINE allows you to search for a specific answer, cut and paste code, download chapters, and stay current with emerging technologies.

Activate your FREE Online Edition at
www.informit.com/safarifree

> **STEP 1:** Enter the coupon code: OIEHTZG.

> **STEP 2:** New Safari users, complete the brief registration form. Safari subscribers, just log in.

If you have difficulty registering on Safari or accessing the online edition, please e-mail customer-service@safaribooksonline.com